Human Body Encyclopedia

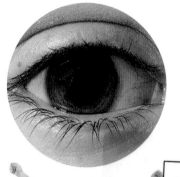

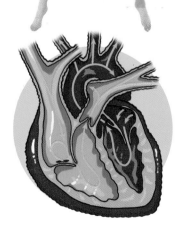

A DORLING KINDERSLEY BOOK

LONDON, NEW YORK, MUNICH,
MELBOURNE, and DELHI

Senior editor Penny Smith
Senior art editor Cheryl Telfer

Editors Ben Morgan, Zahavit Shalev
Additional design Jacqueline Gooden,
Tory Gordon-Harris, Claire Patane, Laura Roberts
Illustrator Peter Bull
Digital illustrator Pilar Morales

Consultants Dr Penny Preston, Dr Frances Williams

Publishing manager Sue Leonard
Managing art editor Clare Shedden
Jacket design Victoria Harvey
Picture researchers Marie Ortu, Rob Nunn
Production controller Shivani Pandey
DTP designer Almudena Díaz

First published in Great Britain in 2005 by
Dorling Kindersley Limited
80 Strand, London WC2R 0RL

A Penguin Company

4 6 8 10 9 7 5 3

Copyright © 2005 Dorling Kindersley Limited, London

A catalogue record for this book
is available from the British Library.

ISBN 1-4053-0848-6

Colour reproduction by Colourscan, Singapore
Printed and bound in China by Toppan

Discover more at
www.dk.com

Contents

Human body

Skeleton and bones

Moving muscles

Brain and senses

Test yourself with the questions at the bottom of each page...

Circles show close-up images you might not otherwise be able to see.

Coloured discs contain facts about special topics, such as taste.

"Get into it" activity buttons show you how you can try things out for yourself.

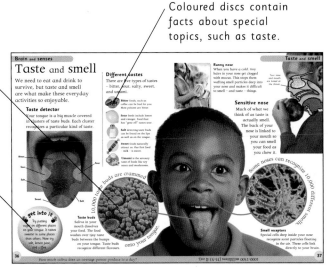

About this book

This book has special features that will show you how to get your hands on as much information as possible! Use the "become an expert" buttons to find out more about a subject on other pages.

Your amazing body

The greatest machine you'll ever own is your body. It's more complicated than any computer, it lasts for a lifetime, and it's yours for free.

Become an expert... on the skeleton, pages **12-13** on digestion, pages **82-83**

Body parts

Your body is made up of hundreds of different parts. You probably know the names of the bits you can see, but there are many more hidden deep inside you.

Hair

Forehead

Ears

Eyebrows

Cheeks

Nose

Eyes

Lips

Teeth

Inside your body

Doctors can see inside your body with special cameras. X-ray cameras take pictures of hard body parts like bones. Other cameras, called scanners, can see soft body parts.

Hands

Wrists

Fingers

Two of everything

Body parts often come in pairs. You have two feet, two eyes, two ears, two lungs, and so on. This means you have a handy spare in case one of them gets damaged.

A chest X-ray shows the bones in your chest. The white shape in the middle is the heart.

What do we call the study of the human body?

Water, water
Water is the most important chemical in your body. About two-thirds of your weight is water.

Curiosity quiz
Take a look at the first few pages in this book and see if you can find these pictures.

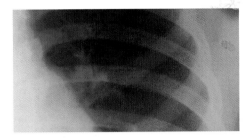

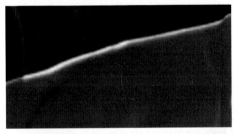

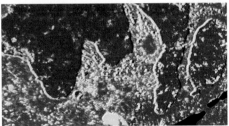

Robot

The ingredients
Your body is made of just a few simple chemicals, plus water.

 Carbon is the chemical in diamonds and coal. A fifth of you is carbon.

 Iron makes your blood red. You have enough to make one small iron nail.

 Phosphorus is in the tips of matches, as well as your bones and teeth.

Sodium and **chlorine** make salt. Blood is one-third as salty as sea water.

 Potassium is used in some types of soap. It's also in your body fluids.

 Nitrogen is important in muscles. It's also the main ingredient in air.

No substitute
The human body is too complicated for robots to copy. Robots can copy the way we walk, but they can't think or feel like we do.

Chimps have hands like ours.

Compared to chimps, our bodies look almost hairless.

Chimpanzee

Being human
Although we look different to animals, our bodies are similar on the inside. Our closest animal relatives are chimpanzees.

What makes you you?

All human bodies work the same way, but everyone is different. Nobody looks, sounds, or thinks exactly like you. You're different because of the way your genes and experience shape you as you grow up.

Fair skin

Green eyes

Curly hair

Black hair

Freckles

Unique

The shape of your face, the colour of your hair, and many other things make you unique – different from everyone else.

How many genes are there in the human body?

In the genes

Genes are instructions that build your body and tell it how to work. Your genes control many of the things that make you unique, like the colour of your eyes or how tall you'll be.

This girl has a gene that allows her to roll up her tongue. The boy doesn't have the gene, so he can't roll his tongue.

There's enough DNA inside you to stretch to the Sun and back 400 times.

DNA

Your genes are stored in a chemical called DNA, which looks like a twisted ladder with four different types of rung. The rungs make up a four-letter alphabet that spells out your genes, like letters in a book.

DNA can split and copy itself.

get into it

Look in a mirror and see if you can roll your tongue. Don't cheat by squeezing it with your lips. Test your family to see who has the gene.

In the family

Your genes came from your parents. Half come from your mother and half come from your father. If you look like your parents, it's because you share the same genes.

Learning to ride a bike changes your brain and your body.

Changing body

Genes don't control everything – experience also shapes you. If you exercise a lot, for instance, your body gets stronger.

Building blocks

Every part of your body is made of tiny building blocks called cells, which fit together like bricks in a wall. Cells are so small that hundreds could fit on the point of a pin.

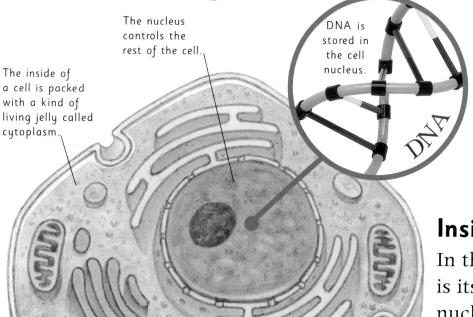

The nucleus controls the rest of the cell.

DNA is stored in the cell nucleus.

DNA

The inside of a cell is packed with a kind of living jelly called cytoplasm.

The skin on your fingertips is made of lots of small ridges.

The outer skin, or membrane, stops things leaking out.

Tiny generators provide cells with power.

Inside a cell

In the middle of a cell is its control centre – the nucleus. The nucleus sends instructions to the rest of the cell, telling the cell what chemicals to make.

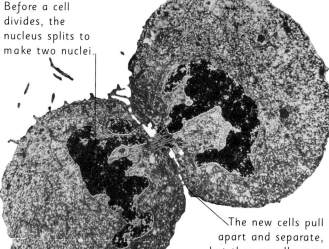

Before a cell divides, the nucleus splits to make two nuclei.

The new cells pull apart and separate, but they usually stay close neighbours.

Making new cells

A cell makes new cells by dividing. The two new cells are half the size, but they soon grow back. Millions of your cells die every second, but millions of others divide to replace them.

How many cells are there in the human body?

How big are cells?

Cells are too small to see with the naked eye, but scientists can photograph them through powerful microscopes. The cells on your skin are about a hundredth of a millimetre wide.

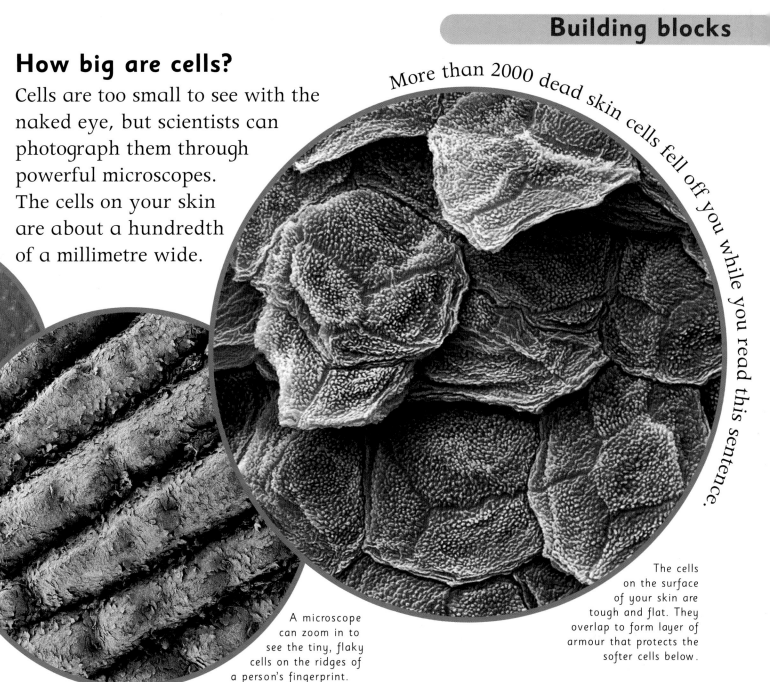

More than 2000 dead skin cells fell off you while you read this sentence.

The cells on the surface of your skin are tough and flat. They overlap to form layer of armour that protects the softer cells below.

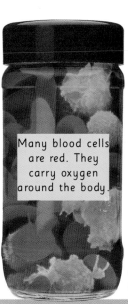

A microscope can zoom in to see the tiny, flaky cells on the ridges of a person's fingerprint.

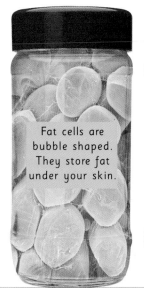
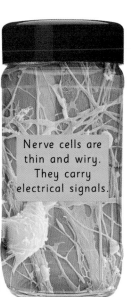
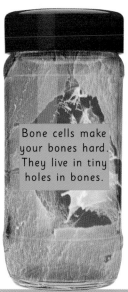

Fat cells are bubble shaped. They store fat under your skin.

Many blood cells are red. They carry oxygen around the body.

Nerve cells are thin and wiry. They carry electrical signals.

Bone cells make your bones hard. They live in tiny holes in bones.

Cells make tissue

Your body contains hundreds of different types of cells that do different jobs. Cells of the same type usually group together to form tissue. Fat, muscle, bone, and nerves are types of tissue. Blood is a liquid tissue.

Organizing the body

Your cells and tissues are organized into larger body parts called organs. In turn, your organs work together to form body systems.

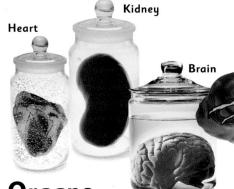

Heart

Kidney

Brain

Organs

An organ is a body part that does a specific job. Your heart's job, for instance is to pump blood. Kidneys clean blood.

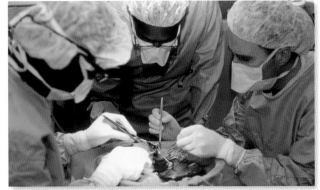

Organ transplant

If a vital organ stops working, doctors may replace it with an organ from another person. This is called a transplant.

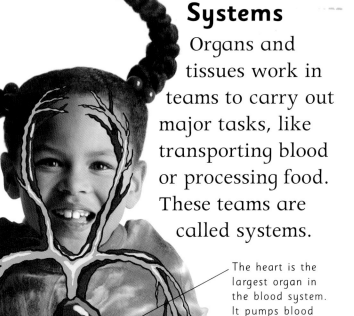

Systems

Organs and tissues work in teams to carry out major tasks, like transporting blood or processing food. These teams are called systems.

The heart is the largest organ in the blood system. It pumps blood around the body.

The tubes that carry blood away from the heart are called arteries (shown in red).

The tubes that carry blood back to the heart are called veins (shown in blue).

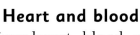

Heart and blood

Your heart, blood, and blood vessels make up the blood system. It transports vital supplies around your body.

Which body system makes your stomach rumble?

Muscles

Your muscle system is made of tissues that move parts of your body by pulling on them or squeezing them. Your biggest muscles all pull on bones.

Your fingers are moved by muscles in your arm.

Muscles change the position of your skeleton by pulling different bones.

The most powerful muscles are in your legs.

Skeleton

Bones and joints make up the skeletal system, an inner frame that supports the body.

A quarter of your bones are in your feet.

Nerves

Your nervous system carries electrical signals around your body. You need this system to see, hear, think, and react.

Signals shoot along nerves to muscles, telling them when to pull.

Senses, such as touch, rely on nerve cells that send signals to your brain.

Your brain is the nervous system's control centre.

Other systems

Some of your other important systems are shown in this list.

Breathing system: the main organs are your lungs, which take in air.

Hormone system: this uses powerful chemicals to control your body and mood.

Skin, hair, and nails: these form your body's protective covering.

Immune system: this seeks and destroys germs that get into your body.

Urinary system: this cleans blood and gets rid of waste chemicals.

Reproductive system: these are the organs that make babies.

Digestive system

Your digestive organs break down food to provide your body with energy and raw materials.

Your mouth is the first part of the digestive system.

A long, twisting tube makes up your intestines, where digested food is absorbed.

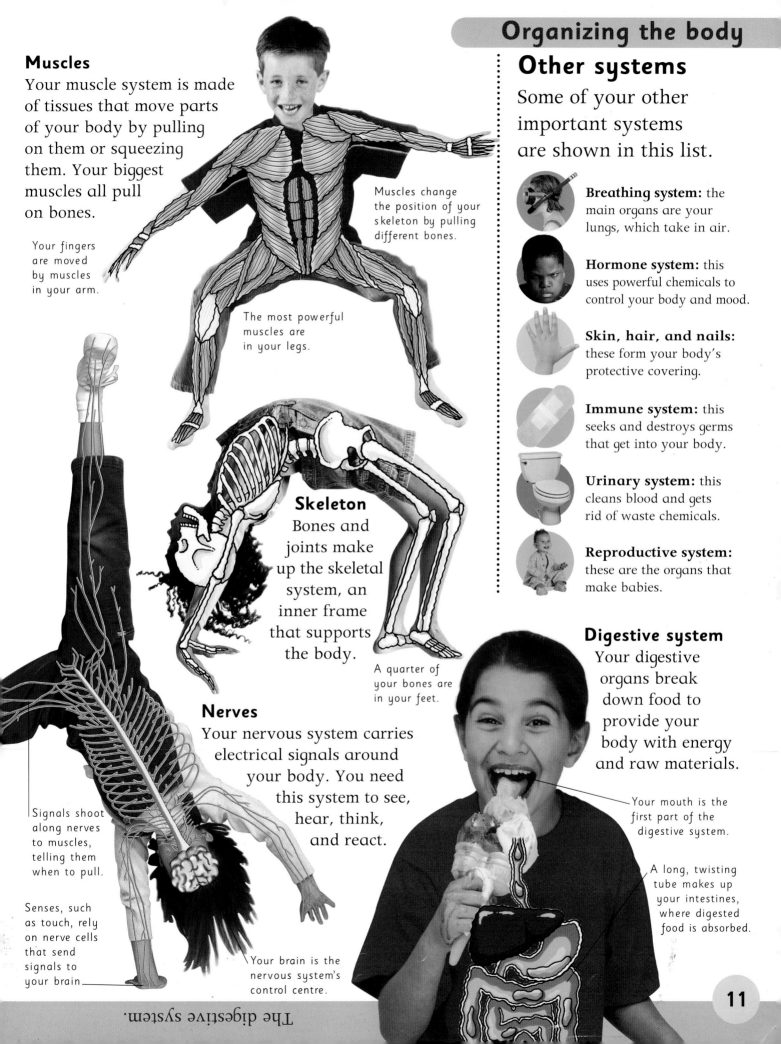

The digestive system.

Skeleton

Your bones all join up to make a frame for your body called the skeleton. This protects your insides, and helps you move about.

Smallest bone

Around the same length as a grain of rice, this is one of the smallest bones in your body. It lies deep inside your ear.

A giraffe's long neck helps it to eat leaves off tall trees.

Neck bones

Did you know that you have seven bones in your neck, the same number as a giraffe? The top one allows you to move your head up and down, the second lets you rotate it from side to side.

Skull

Jaw bone

Rib

Pelvis

There are 24 bones in your spine.

Shoulder blade

Each finger has three bones, except for your thumb, which has two.

206 bones

There are 206 bones in an adult skeleton. Over half of these are found in the hands and feet – the parts of your body that perform the most complicated movements.

You have eight small bones in each wrist.

How many ribs have you got?

Frogs have very short spines to withstand the strain of the huge leaps they take.

A fish's spine allows it to bend its body from side to side so it can swim smoothly.

Other skeletons

Most animals have a backbone and are called "vertebrates". Animals with no spine, like spiders and bugs, are called "invertebrates".

Snakes are incredibly bendy thanks to many identical vertebrae forming their long spines.

Your tail bone is at the very bottom of your spine.

Thigh bone

Shin bone

Your ankle has three larger bones and four smaller ones.

There are 54 bones in your hands, and 52 in your feet.

The thigh bone is the biggest and strongest in the body.

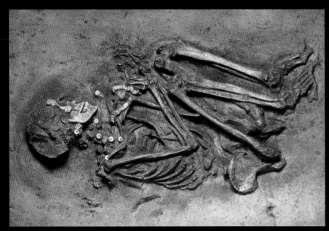

Long lasting
Bone is a very hard material and one of the last parts to rot away when a body is buried. This woman lived in the Stone Age, 5000 years ago, but her bones have survived until today.

Become an expert...
on bone and cartilage, pages 20-21
on teeth, pages 84-85

24, unless you are one of the rare people born with 26.

Head case

The most complex part of the skeleton is the skull. It is made of many bones that fit together tightly, to protect the brain and support the face.

The frontal bone forms your forehead.

The cranium is the domed part of your skull.

Helmet
The upper part of the skull is like a helmet that protects the brain. The lower part forms a structure for your facial features to attach to.

Eye sockets are made up of seven different bones.

The front of the nose has no bones.

The brain fills most of the cranium.

Facial features
This image shows the relationship between your skull and face. There are no bones shaping the front part of your nose, your lips, or your ears. Your nose and ears are shaped by cartilage.

Teeth are set into the upper and lower jaws.

14

Why does a baby have spaces between its cranial bones?

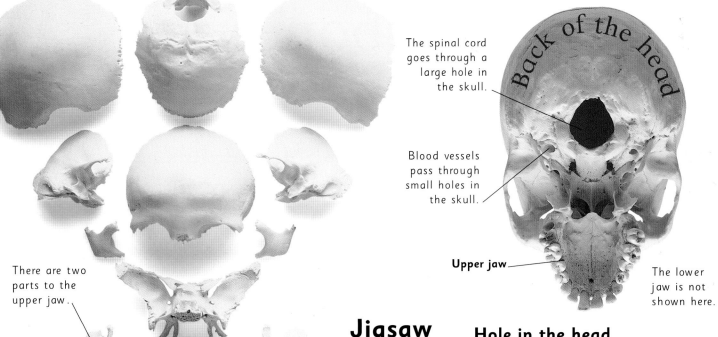

The spinal cord goes through a large hole in the skull.

Blood vessels pass through small holes in the skull.

Back of the head

Upper jaw

The lower jaw is not shown here.

There are two parts to the upper jaw.

The lower jaw is hinged. It is the only skull bone that can move.

Jigsaw

The skull bones fit together like the pieces of a jigsaw. All but one of the bones are locked in place. This makes the skull very strong.

Hole in the head

From underneath you can clearly see the big hole at the bottom of this skull. The spinal cord – which runs down your back – meets your brain here.

Face from the past

Scientists can work out what a dead person's face looked like from their skull alone. They examine the facial bones and build up artificial cartilage, muscle, and skin over them.

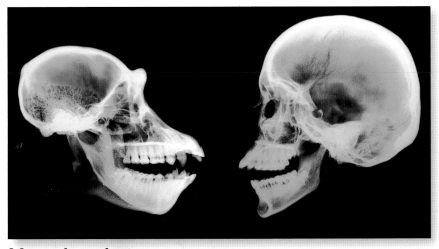

Meet the relatives

Chimpanzees and humans share a common ancestor. However, chimps have smaller brains than humans so their craniums are smaller. Chimps also have a large ridge above their eyes, and a jutting jaw.

So its head could withstand being squashed while it was being born.

Bendy backbone

Your spine is a length of bones running down the back of your body. Without it you couldn't hold up your head and body, or make any sort of movement.

Your spine curves gently, a bit like the letter "s".

The first seven bones are in your neck. They are known as the cervical vertebrae.

The next 12 are called the thoracic vertebrae.

The five lumbar vertebrae bear most of your weight.

The five sacral vertebrae are fused together.

The coccyx consists of four fused vertebrae.

Stack of bones

Your spine contains 24 separate bones called vertebrae. At the bottom are nine more vertebrae. They are much smaller and are fused together.

The thoracic vertebrae form joints with the ribs.

A straight back is actually quite curvy.

The fused bones of the sacrum and coccyx don't allow much movement.

Back of spine

Front of spine

The spinal cord goes through this hole.

Segments of the spine

Each vertebra has a strong, stubby section that supports the weight of your body, and a hole for the spinal cord to pass through.

What is a slipped disc?

Shock absorbers

You twist and bend your spine almost every time you move. Sandwiched between the vertebrae are pads of cartilage to stop them banging and rubbing against each other and getting worn out.

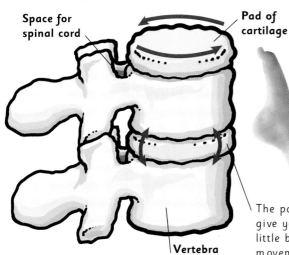

Space for spinal cord

Pad of cartilage

The pads give you a little bit of movement in all directions.

Vertebra

Ribcage

Your thoracic vertebrae connect to your ribs. Together they form a cage around your heart and lungs. Rib bones are curved. They are also thinner and more bendy than the bones in your spine.

A woman's pelvis is shaped differently to a man's. A baby can pass through it when she gives birth.

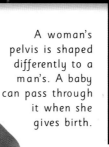

Pelvis

Reproductive organs and some digestive organs rest in the bowl-shaped hollow of your pelvis. The sacral vertebrae and coccyx form the bottom of the bowl.

You could be this bendy.....

The way the back curves means we can't bend as far back as we can forwards.

Bendy backbone

The amount of movement between each vertebra and its neighbours is actually very small, but added together they allow for a large range of movement.

...with a lot of practice!

get into it
Bend over. Gently feel the bones of your spine with your fingertips. Can you follow them from neck to waist?

17

It's when one of the pads between the vertebrae gets damaged.

Living bone

Their outer surface may be hard and dry but that doesn't mean your bones aren't alive. Bones are always growing and repairing themselves.

What's inside our bones?

Bone accounts for one sixth of your body's weight. Its clever structure means it's often lighter than it looks.

Marrow can be found in the spine, skull, and the main leg and arm bones.

Spongy bone

Parts of some bones have a honeycomb structure with lots of spaces. This makes them weigh less than if they were solid right through.

Bone marrow

A jellyish substance called marrow fills the centre of many of your larger bones. It supplies your body with red blood cells at a rate of 3 million cells per second.

Compact bone

The hardest and most dense part of the bones is the outer layer. It is made of calcium, a substance we get from our food. Teeth are made of calcium too.

What are the most commonly broken bones?

Broken bone

Bones are strong and flexible enough to cope with a lot of pressure, but, as this X-ray shows, they sometimes break. Luckily they can heal themselves.

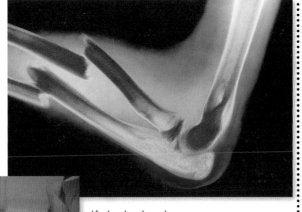

If the broken bone ends have slipped apart they must be repositioned by a doctor before healing begins.

On the mend

New cells form at each end of the broken bone, closing the gap between them. It takes about 6 weeks for this to happen.

Your bones are still growing until your late teens.

Padded clothes help protect bones from sudden impact.

Curiosity quiz

Take a look through the skeleton and bones pages and see if you can identify where these bony bits come from.

Become an expert...
on the skeleton, pages **12-13** on skin and pages **70-71**

Looking after your bones

Calcium from milk and cheese is needed to build strong bones. Weight-bearing exercise like walking, climbing, or skating helps to strengthen bones.

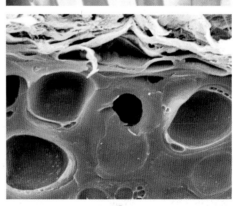

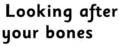

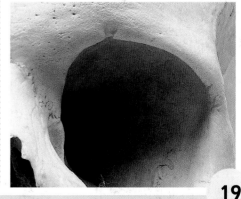

Bone and cartilage

When you were a baby, you were tiny. Slowly, as you get older and bigger, your bones do a clever trick. Not only do they grow, but they also change.

Baby's hand

Making bones

Babies' bones are made out of a soft and bendy material called cartilage. Slowly this hardens and turns into bone.

Baby bones are entirely made of soft, growing cartilage.

Adolescent bones are mostly bone, with a small amount of cartilage.

Adult bones have stopped growing. Most no longer contain cartilage.

More, less

You've got more bones than your mum or dad!

You were born with over 300 "soft" bones, but as you get older, many fuse together. By the time you're 25 you'll have 206 fully formed bones.

Cross-section of an ear – the cartilage sits between two layers of skin.

Stick out your ears!

Your ears are made of cartilage, not bone. They are strong, but much more bendy than your bony bits.

Which foods are rich in calcium, the mineral you need to grow healthy bones?

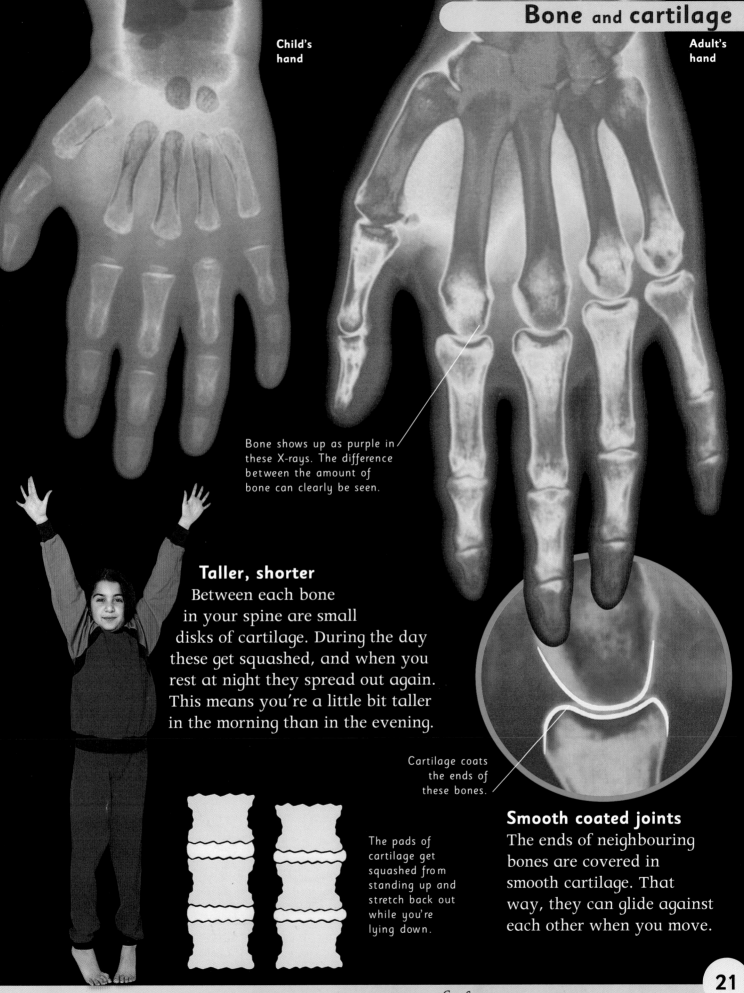

Child's hand

Adult's hand

Bone shows up as purple in these X-rays. The difference between the amount of bone can clearly be seen.

Taller, shorter

Between each bone in your spine are small disks of cartilage. During the day these get squashed, and when you rest at night they spread out again. This means you're a little bit taller in the morning than in the evening.

Cartilage coats the ends of these bones.

The pads of cartilage get squashed from standing up and stretch back out while you're lying down.

Smooth coated joints

The ends of neighbouring bones are covered in smooth cartilage. That way, they can glide against each other when you move.

Moving joints

Joints are the places where bones meet. Different kinds of joints allow you to move in different ways.

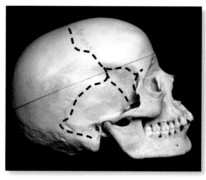

Hinge joint

Your knee can bend in the middle but it can't swing from side to side. This joint has a hinge like the one that allows you to open and close a door.

Knee joint

Fixed joints

The bones that make up your skull start to join up soon after you are born. Once they have fused, none of them allow movement except the hinged jaw joint.

Have you ever used a joystick? That's a ball and socket joint!

Ball and socket

Your hips are ball and socket joints. They allow you to move your legs in all directions and even to turn them.

There are 19 moveable joints in your hand — not counting the ones in your wrist!

What is tennis elbow?

Bendy bits

Different sorts of joints all over your body keep you moving.

 Neck bones feature a pivot joint that allows your head to turn.

 Wrists have a joint that allows them to turn but not to go right round.

 Ankles contain different joints for up and down and side to side movement.

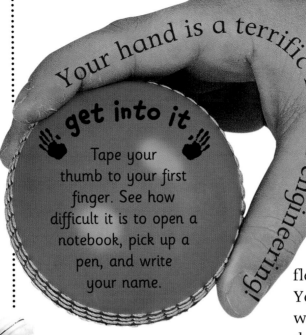

Your hand is a terrific feat of engineering!

get into it

Tape your thumb to your first finger. See how difficult it is to open a notebook, pick up a pen, and write your name.

Thank your thumbs

Your thumb is the most flexible of your fingers. You rely on your thumbs whenever you handle delicate objects.

Hip hooray

Joints, particularly knee and hip joints, sometimes wear out in old age. When this happens, doctors can remove the worn-out joint and replace it with an artificial one.

This woman has stretchy muscles and ligaments that allow her spine to bend further than most people can manage.

Ligaments

Bands of tissue called ligaments act like elastic. They hold your bones together yet still allow you to move.

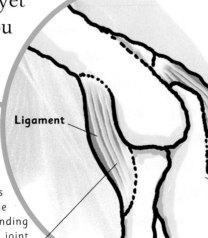

Ligament

Bone

Your elbows have a hinge joint for bending and a pivot joint so they can turn.

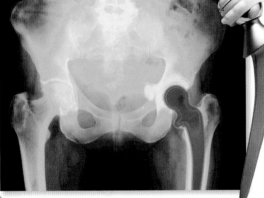

Fabulously flexible

People whose joints are particularly flexible are called "double-jointed". The condition can run in families, but people who are double-jointed must practise if they want to keep their ligaments stretchy.

The name for sore elbow tendons caused by overuse.

The body's muscles

Every time you move, you use muscles. Muscles make you walk, blink, and smile. Some muscles work without you thinking about them, but others need to be told to move. They all work by shrinking, which makes them pull or squeeze.

Pulling strings

About 650 of your muscles are wrapped around the bones of your skeleton. They move your body by pulling on the bones. Together they form the muscle system.

Smooth muscle
This type of muscle makes things move inside your body. It mixes food in your stomach and pushes food through your intestines.

Smooth muscle cells are short with pointed ends.

Heart muscle
When you put your hand on your chest, you can feel your heart beating. Your heart is a strong muscle that squeezes blood around your body.

Heart muscle cells are stripy with oval blobs.

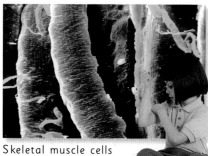

Skeletal muscle
Skeletal muscles pull on bones to change the shape of your skeleton and move your body. These muscles are voluntary, which means you can use thought to control them.

Skeletal muscle cells are long and threadlike.

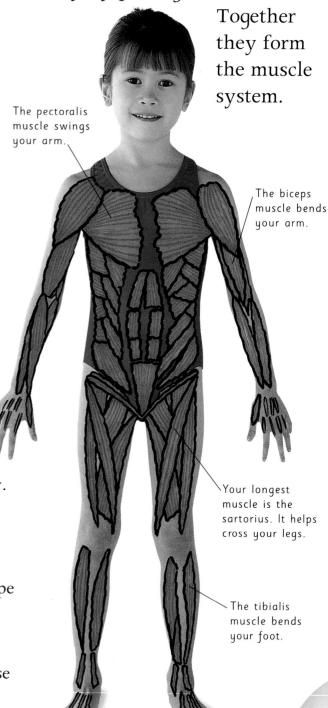

The pectoralis muscle swings your arm.

The biceps muscle bends your arm.

Your longest muscle is the sartorius. It helps cross your legs.

The tibialis muscle bends your foot.

What weighs more: all your bones or all your muscles?

Muscle magic

Muscles have hundreds of uses. They make up about a third of your body weight.

Largest muscle: you use the muscle in your buttock for sitting and walking.

Fastest muscle: this one makes you blink. It works up to 5 times a second.

Ear wiggling: a few people can control the muscles around their ears.

Smile: a fake smile uses different muscles from a real, involuntary smile.

Who's in charge?

You use hundreds of muscles when you run and jump. Your brain controls them all, a bit like a conductor controlling an orchestra. It sends signals along nerves to every muscle, saying exactly when to work and when to rest.

Become an expert ...

on making sounds, pages **64-65**
on how intestines push food, pages **88-89**

Hundreds of muscles work in a carefully controlled sequence when you jump in the air.

Tongue twister

Your tongue is a bundle of lots of muscles that make it super flexible. It can reach anywhere in your mouth to pull and push bits of food. Its acrobatic movements are also vital to speech.

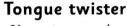

Your tongue contains at least 14 different muscles that make it amazingly flexible.

Your muscles.

25

How muscles work

Muscles work by contracting, which means they shorten. As a muscle contracts, it pulls. The larger the muscle, the more powerfully it pulls.

Working in pairs

Muscles can pull but not push. They work in pairs that pull in opposite directions. When one muscle pulls, its partner relaxes.

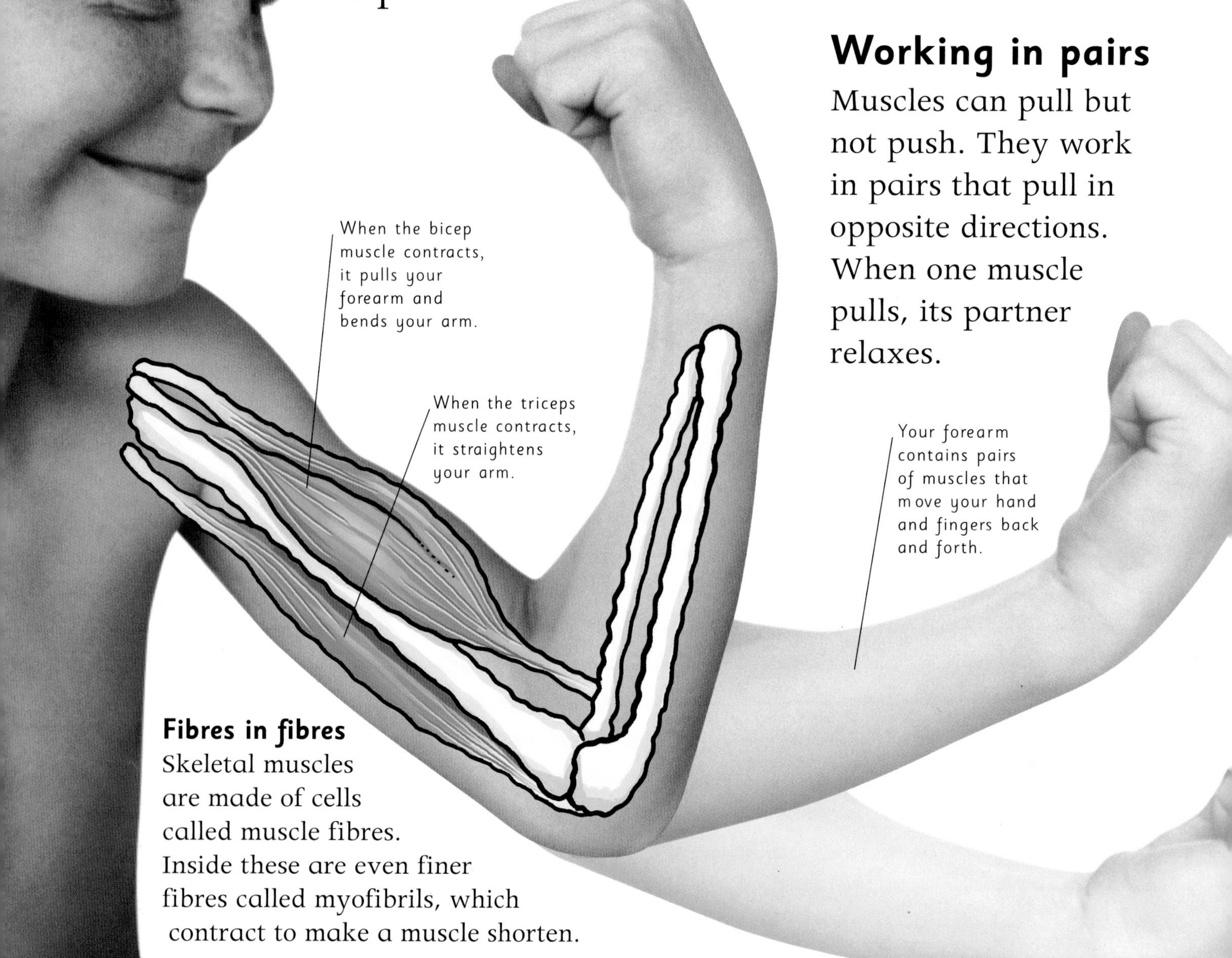

When the bicep muscle contracts, it pulls your forearm and bends your arm.

When the triceps muscle contracts, it straightens your arm.

Your forearm contains pairs of muscles that move your hand and fingers back and forth.

Fibres in fibres

Skeletal muscles are made of cells called muscle fibres. Inside these are even finer fibres called myofibrils, which contract to make a muscle shorten.

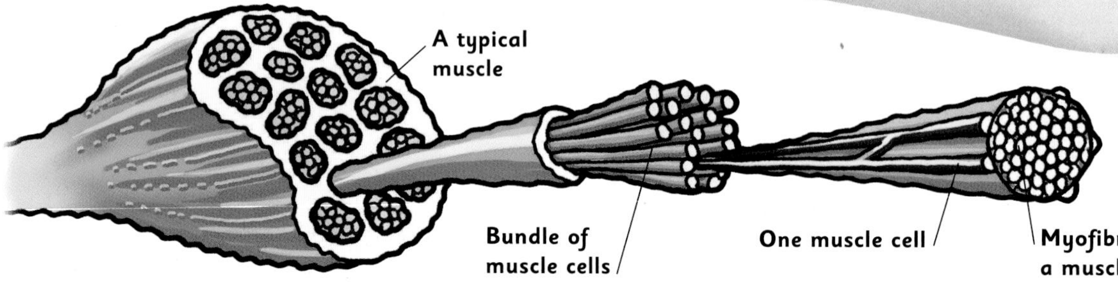

A typical muscle

Bundle of muscle cells

One muscle cell

Myofibrils inside a muscle cell

Where is the body's smallest muscle?

Try raising your ring finger with your hand in this position. It's stuck because it's joined to the same tendon as the middle finger.

Middle finger

Ring finger

Tendons

Muscles are fastened to bones by tough bands called tendons. When you wiggle your fingers, you can see the tendons move on the back of your hand.

Making faces

Muscles in your face are attached to skin as well as bone. They pull the skin when you change your expression. You use about 17 muscles when you smile.

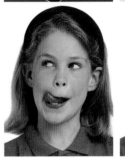
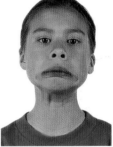

A floppy start

A newborn baby has little control over his head or neck muscles. It takes about a month before it can hold up its head, and six months for strong, steady head control.

No rest

Muscles work all the time. They hold you upright - without them you would flop on the floor. Muscles also work when you are asleep, keeping your body firm and toned.

Getting a stitch

If you run a lot, you may get a pain in your side. This is a stitch. Scientists aren't sure exactly why it happens but it might be because the muscles and ligaments in your abdomen are working too hard.

In the ear.

27

Muscle power

The more you use your muscles, the better they get. Active games and exercise make your muscles larger, stronger, and more flexible. They also help you keep going without tiring.

Stamina

If you have stamina, you can keep going for a long time without getting tired. Exercise that makes you feel out of breath, like running, improves your stamina.

Flexibility

When you're flexible, your joints and muscles can move freely and your body can bend and straighten easily. Exercise that stretches your body, such as gymnastics or dancing, improves your flexibility.

This contortionist has made her body more flexible by doing exercises that stretch her back.

Strength

Pushing, pulling, and lifting make your muscles bigger and stronger. Bodybuilders lift heavy weights over and over again until their muscles are enormous.

You need strong muscles to win a tug-of-war.

Become an expert ...

on how your heart works, pages **50-51**
on healthy food, pages **106-107**

What happens to muscles if you don't exercise?

Muscle food

To build strong muscles, you need a type of food called protein. Meat, fish, beans, milk, and eggs are rich in protein.

Most vegetables don't contain much protein.

Milk

Chicken

Fish

Egg

Beans

Fish is a very good source of protein.

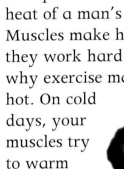

Body heat

This picture shows the heat of a man's body. Muscles make heat when they work hard, which is why exercise makes you hot. On cold days, your muscles try to warm you up by shivering.

Ways to keep fit

Exercise is very good for your health. As well as making your muscles bigger, it strengthens your heart and lungs.

Walking to school, or going out for walks, builds strength and stamina.

Football is great for improving your flexibility and strength.

Swimming strengthens your heart muscle and builds stamina.

Cycling strengthens your leg muscles and builds up stamina.

Dancing keeps your body supple and helps build strength.

They get small and weak.

Headquarters

The brain is the body's control centre. It is a complicated organ that works very quickly, a bit like a brilliant, living computer.

Sense signals
The cerebrum is the main part of your brain. It gets and stores sense information and also controls your movements.

Cerebrum

Clever calculator
The cerebrum is also responsible for thinking, speaking, and complicated tasks such as sums.

Cerebellum

Your brain stem works at the same rate whether you're awake or asleep.

Brain stem

Muscle control
Your cerebellum helps you to balance and move your muscles. You use this bit of your brain when you dance.

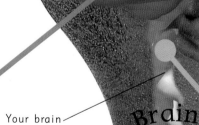

24 hours a day
Whatever else you do, the brain stem makes sure your heart and breathing never stop.

Does your brain hurt when you have a headache?

Skull

Brain

In relation to the size of our bodies, humans have the biggest brains of any animal.

Brain box

Your skull is a bony shell that fits together like a jigsaw around your brain. Shock-absorbing liquid fills the space between the brain and skull.

Learning

When you learn to do something you create connections between cells in your brain. Next time you do it the connections are already there so it is easier.

Short-term memory

Your short-term memory only holds information for about a minute. You use it to compare prices when you go shopping, or to remember a name when you meet someone new.

Long-term memory

Your name, phone numbers you know by heart, and skills such as riding a bike can be kept for many years in your long-term memory.

Curiosity quiz

Take a look through the brain and senses pages and see if you can spot where these come from.

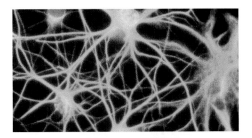

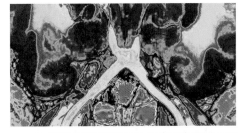

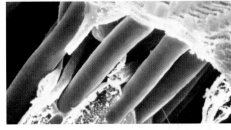

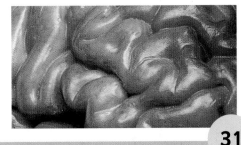

No, your brain can't feel pain but the muscles around your head can.

31

Network of nerves

All of the body contains nerve cells. These link up to form the network of nerves we call the nervous system. It transports messages between the body and the brain.

Quick as a flash

Nerve cells lie next to one another forming long chains. They pass messages to their neighbours – rather like a speedy relay race – to and from the brain.

A good night's sleep

Your body and brain slow down when you sleep, but they don't stop working. Your brain needs sleep to sort out the events of the previous day.

Your knee jumps forwards even though your brain hasn't told it to move.

Cross your legs and tap just below the knee.

No need to think

You do some things without needing to think about them. These are called reflex actions and include blinking, coughing, and the knee-jerk reflex.

Brain

Spinal cord – the centre of the network

Brain cells viewed through a microscope.

Which is the longest nerve in your body?

Pain-killers

When you get a filling, the dentist gives you an anaesthetic. This drug stops nerves passing on pain messages for a short time.

Pins and needles

Sitting cross-legged for a long time squashes the nerves in your legs. When you stand up, the nerves start to work again, producing a tingling feeling.

You've got 150,000 km (93,200 miles) of nerves in your body.

Messages

Your brain controls your body. It receives messages from all parts of your body and decides what to do.

Messages travel faster than a high-speed train.

Walking is the result of your brain telling your leg muscles to move.

Hunger is your stomach telling your brain that it's empty and you must eat.

Needing to urinate is a response to the message that your bladder is full.

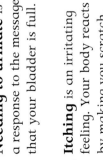

Itching is an irritating feeling. Your body reacts by making you scratch.

Pain gets a very quick response. You move away from what's hurting you.

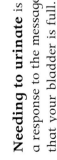

Blinking happens without you needing to think about it.

Breathing is automatic too. It carries on even when you are asleep.

The one running from your big toe to the base of your spine.

Touchy feely

Your skin is in immediate contact with the world. Using your sense of touch allows you to tell if something is hot or cold, dull or sharp, rough or smooth, or wet or dry.

Merkel's disk responds to light touch and is sensitive to the texture of things.

Things we can feel

Skin is packed with many sense receptors. Each sort responds to different sensations.

Warmth is detected by nerve endings quite close to the surface of the skin.

Cold is felt by different sensors to heat. Extreme cold registers as pain.

Deep touch sensors enable you to grip things tightly.

Light touch sensors lie at the root of hairs on your arms and legs.

Vibrations from an electric drill trigger vibration sensors.

Tickly feelings result from a light and unexpected touch.

Sensitive fingertips full of receptors are able to tell coins apart.

Not worth noticing

Although your brain receives messages all the time, it filters out the less important ones. That's why you're not constantly aware of the clothes against your skin.

It feels slimy!....

Meissner's corpuscle senses light touch.

Ouch!

The body has its own system of alarm bells. Pain receptors warn us when a part of the body has been hurt or is about to be harmed.

This girl quickly moves her finger away from the thorn to stop the pain.

How many touch receptors are in a fingertip

Free nerve endings respond to heat, cold, and pain.

The Ruffini ending responds to firm or continuous touch.

Surface of skin

Dermis

Fat

The Pacinian corpuscle responds to firm pressure and vibration.

Under the skin

Dead cells form the surface of your skin. Below that lie sweat glands, hair follicles, and different types of sensory receptors.

.... the message shoots off to the brain....

Sensitive bits

Skin contains more touch receptors than any other part of the body. But some areas are more sensitive than others.

Fingertips are packed with sensors, especially light pressure receptors.

Lips have very thin skin which is good at detecting heat and cold.

Toes are very sensitive, but thick skin makes the heel less sensitive.

Reading by touch

Braille is a system that uses raised dots to represent letters and numbers. It was invented so that people with bad eyesight would be able to read by feeling the page with their fingertips instead of looking at words.

Braille was invented over 150 years ago.

B I R D

get into it
Put one finger in cold water, one in hot, then put both in warm water. The water feels cold to the hot-water finger and hot to the cold-water finger.

About 3,000. That's roughly the same as on the whole of the trunk of your body.

Taste and smell

We need to eat and drink to survive, but taste and smell are what make these everyday activities so enjoyable.

Taste detector

Your tongue is a big muscle covered in clusters of taste buds. Each cluster recognizes a particular kind of taste.

Bitter

Sour

Salt

Sweet

Sour

Salt

Different tastes

There are five types of tastes – bitter, sour, salty, sweet, and umami.

 Bitter foods, such as coffee can be bad for you. Most poisons are bitter.

 Sour foods include lemon and vinegar. Food that has "gone off" tastes sour.

 Salt detecting taste buds can be found on the lips as well as on the tongue.

 Sweet foods naturally attract us. Our first food – milk – is sweet.

 Umami is the savoury taste of foods like soy sauce and mushrooms.

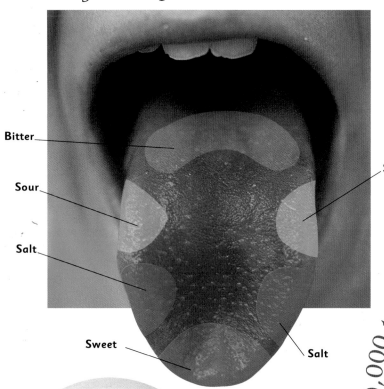

10,000 taste buds are crammed onto your tongue.

get into it
Try putting sugar on different places on your tongue. It tastes sweeter in some places than others. Now try salt, lemon juice, and coffee.

Taste buds
Saliva in your mouth dissolves your food. The food washes over tiny taste buds between the bumps on your tongue. Taste buds recognize different flavours.

How much saliva does an average person produce in a day?

Runny nose

When you have a cold, tiny hairs in your nose get clogged with mucus. This stops them wafting smell particles deep into your nose and makes it difficult to smell – and taste – things.

Your nose and mouth are linked at the throat.

Sensitive nose

Much of what we think of as taste is actually smell. The back of your nose is linked to your mouth so you can smell your food as you chew it.

Some noses can recognize 10,000 different smells.

Smell receptors

Special cells deep inside your nose recognize scent particles floating in the air. These cells link directly to your brain.

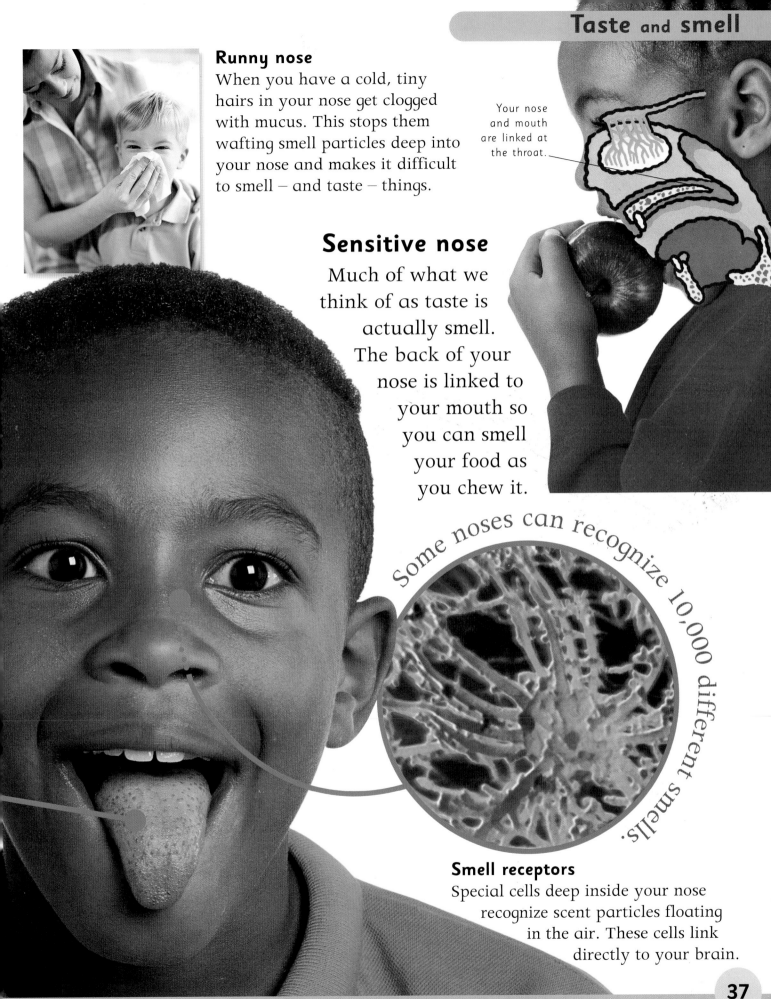

37

Look out!

Sight is the body's main sense and the main way we learn about our surroundings. Two-thirds of the information we take in comes from our eyes.

Wandering eyes

Six muscles control each eye. You use both eyes when you look at something, so your eyes move together.

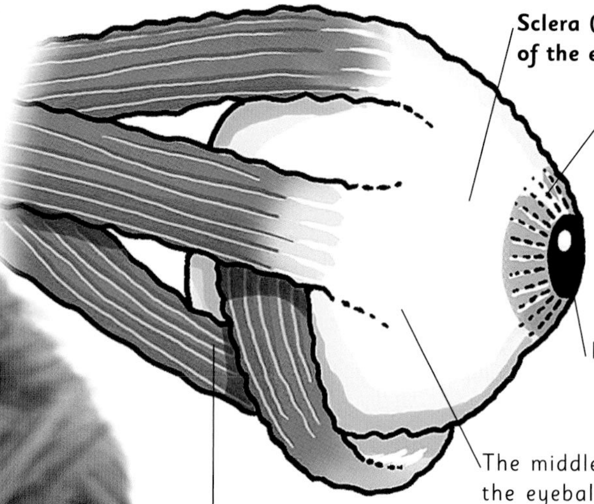

Sclera (or white of the eye)

Iris

Pupil

The middle of the eyeball is filled with fluid.

The muscles surrounding your eyeball make precise movements so you can smoothly track moving objects.

An iris is as unique as a fingerprint

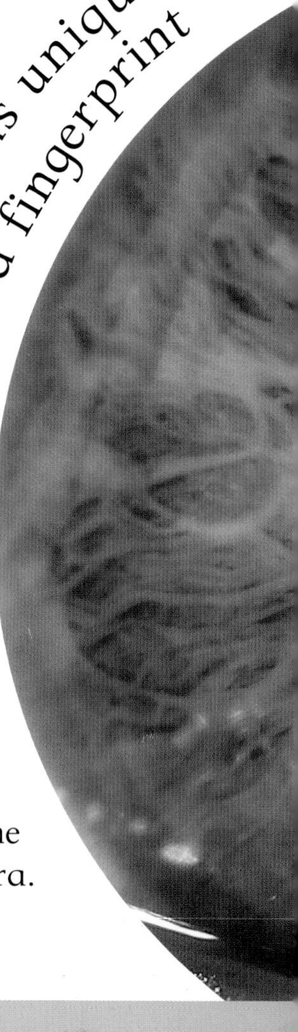

At night, our eyes could detect a lighted candle 1.6 km (1 mile) away.

Pupil

Eyelid

Sclera

Iris

Hidden away

Most of your eye nestles safely in its socket and is protected by pads of fat. On the outside, you can see the iris, pupil, and some of the sclera.

What is the sleep that collects in our eyes?

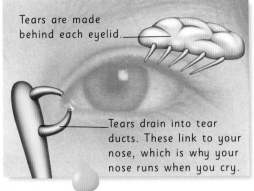

Tears are made behind each eyelid.

Tears drain into tear ducts. These link to your nose, which is why your nose runs when you cry.

Crying

Tear glands behind your eyes produce drops of salty fluid. When you blink, your eyelids sweep this fluid over your eyes to keep them clean. If something gets into your eye, or you feel strong emotions, the drops turn into floods of tears.

Safekeeping

Your eyes are fragile, squidgy balls made of watery jelly so they need to be well protected.

Bone in your skull surrounds your brain and the backs of the eyes.

Eyebrows sit above your eyes and prevent sweat dripping into them.

Eyelids and lashes stop dust entering the eyes and then sweep it well away.

Eye colour

The iris is the coloured part of the eye. All eye colours are produced by one substance, melanin. Lots of melanin results in brown eyes, less means a lighter shade.

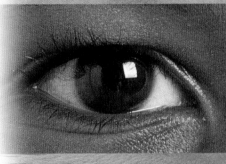

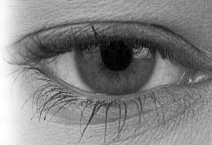

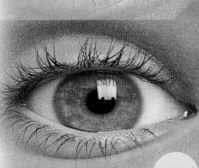

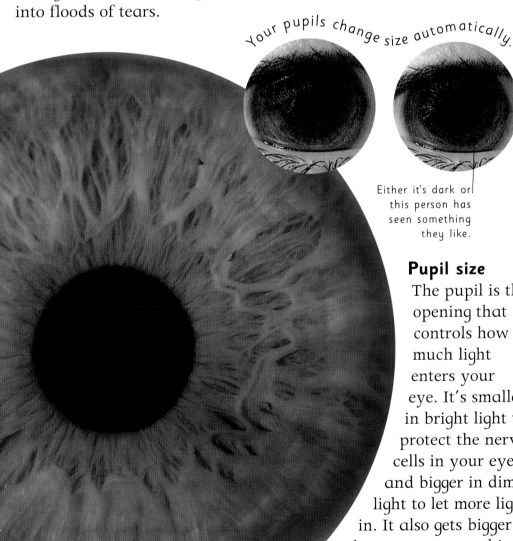

Your pupils change size automatically.

Either it's dark or this person has seen something they like.

Pupil size

The pupil is the opening that controls how much light enters your eye. It's smaller in bright light to protect the nerve cells in your eye, and bigger in dim light to let more light in. It also gets bigger when you see something or someone you like.

Dust and mucus washed from our eyes as we sleep.

How we see

Inside your eye is a lens like the lens of a camera. Its job is to focus light on the back of your eye so you can see things clearly.

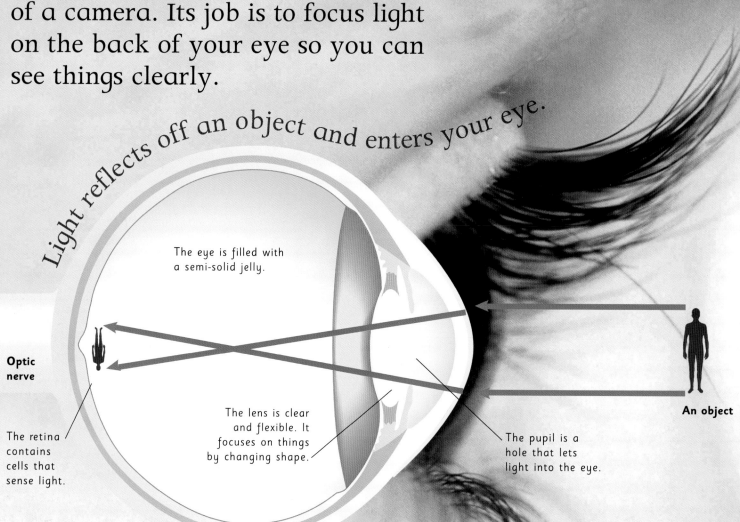

Light reflects off an object and enters your eye.

The eye is filled with a semi-solid jelly.

Optic nerve

The retina contains cells that sense light.

The lens is clear and flexible. It focuses on things by changing shape.

The pupil is a hole that lets light into the eye.

An object

How your eye works

Light from an object enters your eye through the pupil. It passes through the lens, and makes an upside down image on the retina at the back of your eye. Cells in your eye send messages down the optic nerve to your brain. Your brain flips the image back the right way round.

Seeing in colour
Your eyes contain millions of cells. Cone cells give you colour vision but don't work well in dim light. Rod cells work well in dim light but see everything in shades of grey.

What is an eye specialist who tests eyesight called?

Blurry vision

Sometimes an eyeball is the wrong shape. The lens cannot focus light on the retina and everything is blurry. Glasses make the light focus in the right place to make things clear.

Short eyeball

If you have a short eyeball you will have difficulty seeing things close up. This is called long sightedness.

Long eyeball

It is difficult to see objects that are far away when your eyeball is too long. This is known as short sightedness.

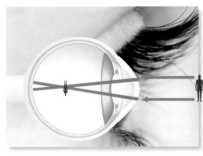

Can you see a number? If not, you may be colour blind.

Colour blindness

Some people cannot tell certain colours apart, especially red and green. This is called colour blindness. It is more common in men than women.

get into it

Close one eye and hold a finger in front of your nose. Open that eye and close the other one. The finger appears to move! Each eye sees things differently.

Contact lenses

These work like mini glasses and sit directly in front of the eye. They're a bit fiddly, but once they're in you can't feel them at all.

Glasses bend the light entering your eye so it focuses on the retina.

Contact lenses are made of very thin plastic.

Eye to brain

Your brain works out what you're seeing by comparing the images it gets from your eyes to things you have seen in the past. Sometimes it can be fooled!

What can you see?

The dark blue in these pictures shows how much animals can see clearly. Light blue shows what they can see less well.

Humans have to move their heads to see clearly to the sides or look back.

Tigers see well to the front to help them find and catch their prey.

Zebras keep a look out for movements to the sides so they can avoid attack.

Ducks can see all the way behind them, even while facing forwards.

Chameleons see small areas clearly. They swivel their eyes to see all around.

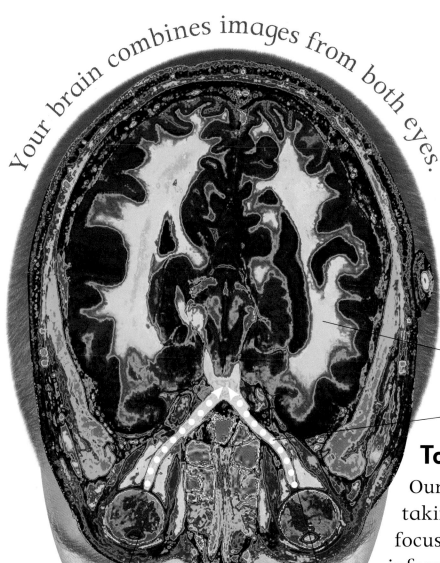

Your brain combines images from both eyes.

The yellow areas are the parts of your brain that deal with information from your eyes.

Optic nerve

Eyeball

Your blind spot is the part of the eye that can't see anything. It is where the optic nerve leaves the back of your eye.

To the brain

Our eyes swivel around constantly, taking in sights and adjusting to focus on different things. The information they collect travels to the brain through the optic nerve at the back of the eyes.

What is it called when you look at something and think it's something else?

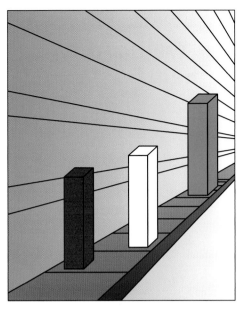

Tallest tower

Does the green tower look taller than the others? That's because it's further along the track and we expect objects further away from us to look smaller. The colours of the towers also affect the size they seem to be. In fact, all the towers are exactly the same size.

Finding your blind spot

Close your right eye and look directly at the star. Slowly bring the book to your left eye. You reach your blind spot when the circle disappears.

Recognizing objects

Your brain is very clever – it can recognize this car from different points of view. A computer would have to be taught that both these pictures are of the same object.

Certain patterns trick your eyes into seeing movement where there is none.

Do you believe your eyes?

Your brain helps your eyes to understand what they see. Sometimes you see things that aren't actually there...

You see a heart even though the edge of the shape isn't there because your brain uses the information it has to fill in the gaps.

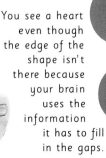

An optical illusion.

Listen here

When you shout you send out
invisible sound waves through
the air. Your ears pick up
the waves and transmit
the sound to your brain.

The speed of sound

We don't notice the slight
delay between someone's
lips moving and
the sound actually
reaching our ears.
It's too fast!

How well can you hear?

Your hearing range is from
the highest to the lowest
notes that you can hear.

Adults have quite a small range compared to other animals.

Children hear higher notes than adults. Your range shrinks with age.

Cats, dogs, and rabbits can hear much higher notes than people.

Bats have excellent hearing. Their range is five times as large as ours.

Sound travels through the

Headphones feed different sounds into each ear so you feel as if you're surrounded by instruments.

Why two ears?

Sounds normally reach one ear
first and then the other. This
helps our brains work out
where sounds are coming from
and how far away they are.

Why do we have ear wax?

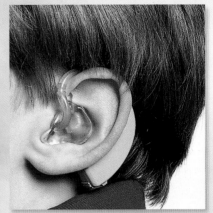

Outer ear

What we call the ear is really just the part that we can see. Sounds are collected here, and funnelled inwards.

A little help

Partially deaf people may use hearing aids. These make the sounds entering the ear louder and easier to hear.

Middle ear

Sounds arriving here from the outer ear cause the eardrum to vibrate and set off movements in three tiny little bones.

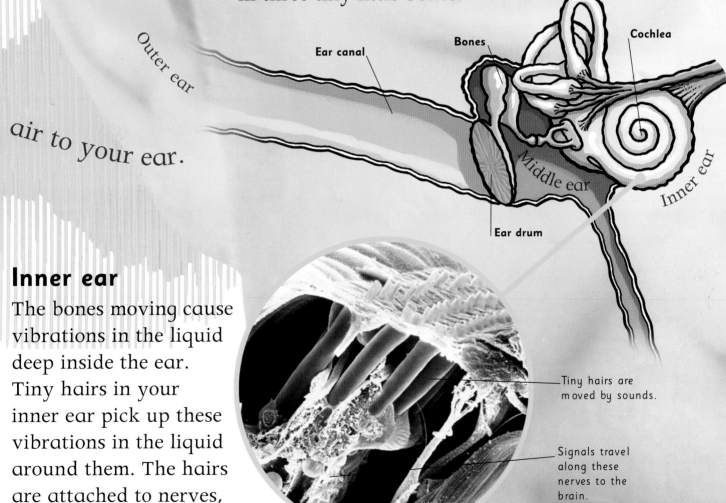

Outer ear

air to your ear.

Ear canal

Bones

Cochlea

Middle ear

Inner ear

Ear drum

Tiny hairs are moved by sounds.

Signals travel along these nerves to the brain.

Inner ear

The bones moving cause vibrations in the liquid deep inside the ear. Tiny hairs in your inner ear pick up these vibrations in the liquid around them. The hairs are attached to nerves, which connect to your brain.

45

To protect the skin lining the ear canal, trap dust, and repel insects.

Balancing act

As well as hearing, ears help you balance. Sensors in your ears work with those in your eyes, muscles, joints, and feet to let your brain know your body's position.

The three semi-circular canals deal with balance.

Ear hole

Keeping track

Deep inside your ear are three tiny tubes filled with fluid. They detect the movements your body is making and let your brain know about them.

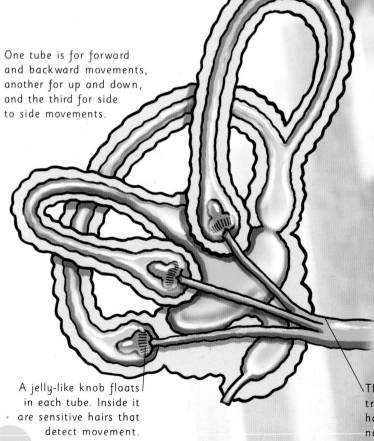

One tube is for forward and backward movements, another for up and down, and the third for side to side movements.

Watch your step!

Keeping your balance while walking along a narrow wall takes a lot of concentration. You are responding to information coming from your eyes, muscles, and ears at the same time.

A jelly-like knob floats in each tube. Inside it are sensitive hairs that detect movement.

The movements travel along the hairs, through a nerve, to the brain.

Can astronauts learn to balance in space?

Motion sickness

Travelling in a car, boat, or plane can make you feel ill. Your eyes tell your brain that you're staying still in the vehicle, but your body says it can feel movement. This confusion is what causes motion sickness.

Basically, your brain is the boss.

Muscle messages

When you move, sensors in your muscles send messages to your brain. If a movement isn't going right, your brain will make you do things differently.

The brain

The more you practise the better you will be at balancing.

get into it

First make sure there is nothing unsafe nearby for you to crash into. Then spin round and round and make yourself feel dizzy.

Why do you feel dizzy?

The liquid in the tubes of your ear is like water in a cup. When you spin, it continues to slosh around for a while even after you've stopped. Your brain gets confused about which way round you are, and you feel dizzy as a result.

47

Yes, but it can take a couple of days to learn how.

Blood flow

Blood is the body's transport system. Pumped by the heart, it travels around the body in tubes called blood vessels, delivering vital supplies to keep your cells alive.

Tube transport

Blood leaves the heart in large blood vessels called arteries, and it returns in vessels called veins. Between the arteries and veins are tiny vessels called capillaries.

Artery

Vein

Capillary

Each major organ has an artery bringing fresh blood and a vein carrying away used blood.

The aorta is the biggest blood vessel in your body. It is as thick as your thumb. A blue whale's aorta is wide enough to swim through!

The vena cava is your biggest vein.

Lung

Lung

Liver

Stomach

Kidney

Kidney

Blood picks up oxygen from the lungs and carries it around the rest of the body.

Around the body

Blood travels round your body, passing through organs on the way. It picks up oxygen in the lungs and food in the liver, then gets rid of waste in the kidneys.

When you cut yourself, what kind of blood vessel does the blood usually come from?

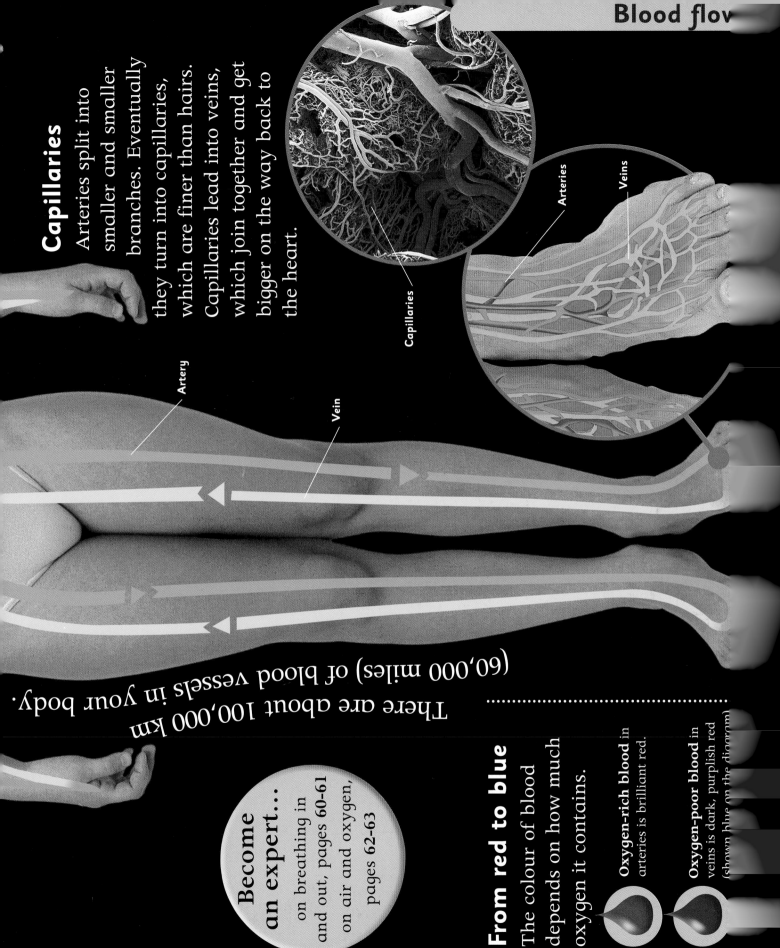

Capillaries

Arteries split into smaller and smaller branches. Eventually they turn into capillaries, which are finer than hairs. Capillaries lead into veins, which join together and get bigger on the way back to the heart.

Capillaries

Arteries

Veins

Artery

Vein

There are about 100,000 km (60,000 miles) of blood vessels in your body.

Become an expert...

on breathing in and out, pages 60-61 on air and oxygen, pages 62-63

From red to blue

The colour of blood depends on how much oxygen it contains.

Oxygen-rich blood in arteries is brilliant red.

Oxygen-poor blood in veins is dark, purplish red (shown blue on the diagram)

A capillary.

Boom boom

Your heart is a pump that pushes blood around your whole body. Each time your heart beats, it squirts out a small cupful of blood and refills for the next beat.

Where is it?

Your heart is in the middle of your chest, squeezed between the two lungs. You can feel its beat just left of the bone in the middle of your chest.

Double pump

Your heart is really two pumps in one. One half pumps blood through your lungs, and the other half pumps blood around the rest of your body.

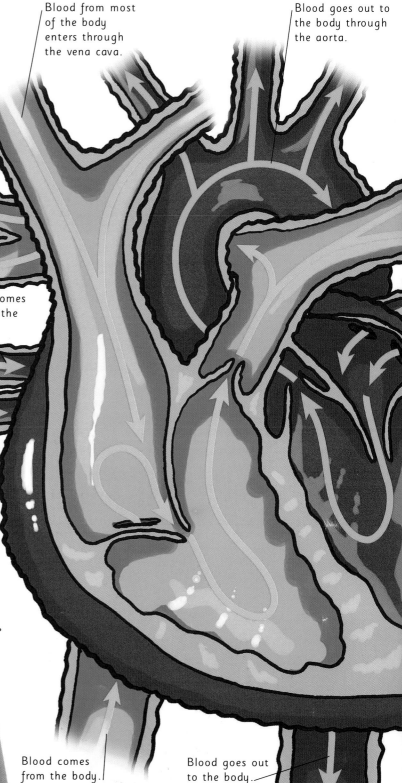

Blood from most of the body enters through the vena cava.

Blood goes out to the body through the aorta.

Blood goes out to the lungs.

Blood comes in from the lungs

One side pumps blood to the lungs...

Blood comes from the body.

Blood goes out to the body.

Vena cava

Aorta

50

How many times does your heart beat in a year?

One-way system

To keep blood flowing one way only, your heart and most veins contain valves. Your heartbeat is the sound of valves shutting when your heart squeezes.

Blood goes out to the lungs.

Blood comes in from the lungs.

Valves stop blood flowing backwards.

...and the other pumps blood everywhere else.

Beating faster

Muscles need extra blood when you're active, so your heart speeds up. It beats about 70 times a minute if you're resting but up to 200 times a minute if you're running.

get into it
Find your pulse by pressing two fingers on your wrist. You should be able to feel a gentle throb as your heart pumps blood around your body.

Curiosity quiz

Take a look through the heart and blood pages and see if you can spot any of the cells and tissues below.

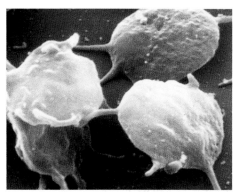

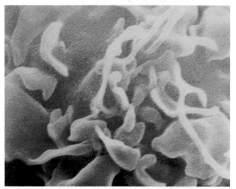

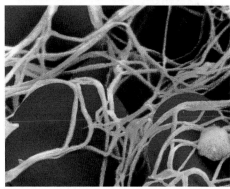

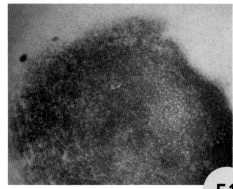

About 40 million times.

All about blood

Blood is a warm, soupy mixture of liquid and cells. The cells carry oxygen and fight germs, and the liquid carries nutrients to body cells and takes away waste.

Main ingredients

Blood contains three types of cells – red blood cells, white blood cells, and platelets. They float in a yellowish liquid called plasma.

One drop of blood contains

5 million red blood cells, half a million platelet cells, 7,000 white blood cells, water, sugar, salt, hormones, vitamins, fat, and protein.

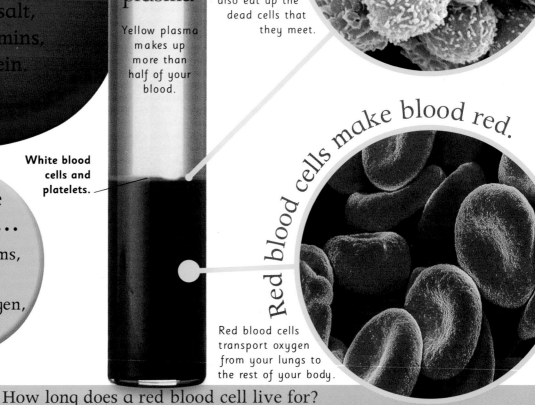

Lots of plasma

Yellow plasma makes up more than half of your blood.

White blood cells seek out and kill germs. They also eat up the dead cells that they meet.

White blood cells and platelets.

Red blood cells make blood red.

Red blood cells transport oxygen from your lungs to the rest of your body.

Become an expert...

on fighting germs, pages **78-79**

on air and oxygen, pages **62-63**

How long does a red blood cell live for?

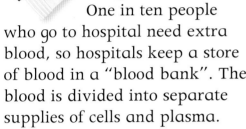

Blood bank

One in ten people who go to hospital need extra blood, so hospitals keep a store of blood in a "blood bank". The blood is divided into separate supplies of cells and plasma.

Your blood type

There are four main types of blood, called blood groups. Your blood group affects who you can donate blood to.

A People with blood group A can give blood only to people with A or AB.

O People with blood group O can donate blood to almost anyone.

AB People with blood group AB can only give blood to others with AB blood.

B People with blood group B can give blood only to people with B or AB.

How much blood?

The average adult has about 10 pints (5.7 litres) of blood, but a newborn baby has only a cupful.

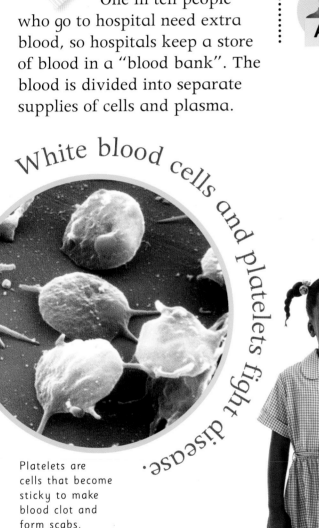

White blood cells and platelets fight disease.

Platelets are cells that become sticky to make blood clot and form scabs.

By a year old a baby has more than 1 pint (half a litre) of blood.

The amount of blood in your body grows with you. By age 10 you have up to 4 pints (2 litres).

Blood cells

Nearly half the cells in your body are blood cells. They wear out quickly, so you make three million new ones every second. Most are made in bone marrow, a jelly-like tissue in hollow bones.

Red blood cells

The most common cells in your body are red blood cells. They are circular with dimples in each side. Inside they are packed with a red protein which carries oxygen and is called haemoglobin.

White blood cell

Tiny tunnels

Red blood cells are soft and rubbery so as to squeeze through tiny gaps. In the smallest blood vessels they travel in single file. All the bumping and squeezing eventually wears them out.

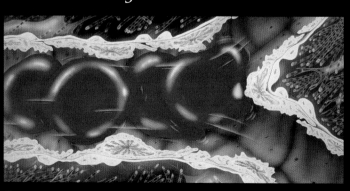

54

Stick together

Platelets are tiny fragments of cells that help blood to clot. They cluster around breaks in blood vessels and grow spiky stalks that help them stick together.

This white blood cell eats pus and germs.

This white blood cell crawls between other cells looking for germs.

Platelets stick together in a blood clot.

Soldier cells

There are lots of different white blood cells and they all help guard your body against invasion by germs. Some white blood cells creep along the walls of blood vessels and eat any germs they find. Others make chemicals that destroy germs.

Thicker blood

When people climb high mountains, their bodies make extra red blood cells to help them breathe in the thin mountain air. As a result, their blood gets thicker.

Pupils are normally black but they look red in photographs taken with a flash.

Seeing red

You can often see people's blood in photographs. If you take a picture with a flash, the light reflects off red blood cells in the back of their eyes, turning the pupils red.

Red blood cells.

Bumps and cuts

Blood has the amazing ability to turn from liquid to solid in minutes and so help mend cuts in your skin.

Clotting

The moment you cut yourself, your blood starts turning solid, or clotting. The clot quickly plugs the broken blood vessels and stops them from leaking.

Caught in a net

The chemicals released by platelets cause tangled fibres to form in the liquid part of blood. The fibres trap blood cells like fish in a net, forming a solid plug that gets bigger and bigger.

Tangled fibres trap blood cells.

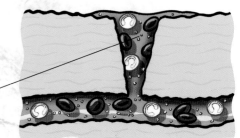

Platelets in action

Platelets start the clotting process. They change shape to become stickier and cluster around the cut. At the same time, they release chemicals into the blood.

Platelets in the blood start to work as soon as you get a cut in your skin.

How long does a small cut take to stop bleeding?

Bloodsucker

A leech is a kind of worm that bites your skin and sucks out your blood. Leech saliva contains chemicals that stops blood from clotting. As a result, the cut keeps bleeding until the leech is full.

Leeches live in wet, swampy places. They often slip down people's shoes and bite their feet without being noticed.

First aid

A plaster can help a cut to heal by closing the skin and keeping out dirt. Plasters also stop you scratching, which can make a cut worse.

Vampire bats and leeches can stop blood from clotting.

Scabs

When a blood clot dries, it forms a scab. New skin slowly grows underneath the scab, repairing the wound. When the skin is ready, the scab becomes loose and drops off.

Scabs keep out germs while new skin grows.

Bumps and cuts

Painful bumps and cuts are a part of your body's natural healing process.

 A graze is a group of tiny cuts. It forms when something rough scrapes the skin quickly.

 Blisters are bubbles of liquid that form when skin is rubbed a lot. Don't pop them!

 Bruises are patches of blood under the skin. They change colour as they heal.

 Black eyes are bruises that form when blood pools under the skin around the eye.

Platelets stick to each other and to other blood cells, causing a clot to start forming.

After a few minutes, the clot is thick enough to stop blood escaping from the wound.

57

Hormones

A hormone is a chemical that changes the way part of your body works. Even tiny amounts of hormones are powerful. Some work slowly over years, but others have instant effects.

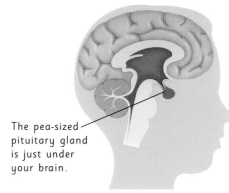

The pea-sized pituitary gland is just under your brain.

Main gland

Hormones are made in parts of the body called glands. The most important is the pituitary gland in your brain. Its hormones control many of the other glands.

Growth hormone

Every day, your pituitary gland releases about eight microscopic doses of growth hormone, mostly when you're asleep. This hormone makes your bones and muscles grow.

The amount of growth hormone you make in one year is less than this tiny pinch of sugar.

Growing up

Toddlers and teenagers have very high levels of growth hormone, which is why they grow so quickly. Adults also make growth hormone, but the level falls with age.

What carries hormones around the body?

Control chemicals

Hormones are important – they control many body processes.

 Oestrogen is the female sex hormone. It turns little girls into adult women.

 Testosterone is the male sex hormone. It turns little boys into adult men.

 Melatonin helps control the daily cycle of sleeping and waking.

 Glucagon raises the level of sugar in your blood, giving you energy.

 Parathyroid hormone tells your bones to release calcium into the blood.

Sugar control

The hormone insulin helps control the level of sugar in your blood. Some people don't make enough insulin and have to check their blood sugar level regularly. They have a disease called diabetes.

People with diabetes prick their skin to get a drop of blood, so they can check how much sugar it contains.

The fright hormone

The hormone adrenaline makes you feel scared or excited. It works in an instant, preparing your whole body for sudden action in case you need to escape from danger.

Adrenaline makes your heart and lungs work harder. Your heart starts to pound and you gasp as your lungs take in extra air.

Your brain becomes alert so you can think quickly.

Become an expert ...

on growing up, pages **102-103**
on sleep, pages **108-109**

Glands above your kidneys release adrenaline.

Your hairs stand on end, making your skin tingle.

Adrenaline travels to your arms and legs and prepares the muscles for action.

Air bags

We have to breathe all the
time in order to supply our
bodies with oxygen and
to get rid of carbon
dioxide. We use our
lungs to do this.

Prepare the air

Before the air reaches your lungs it
travels through your mouth and
nose and then goes down your
windpipe. It gets warm and
damp on its journey.

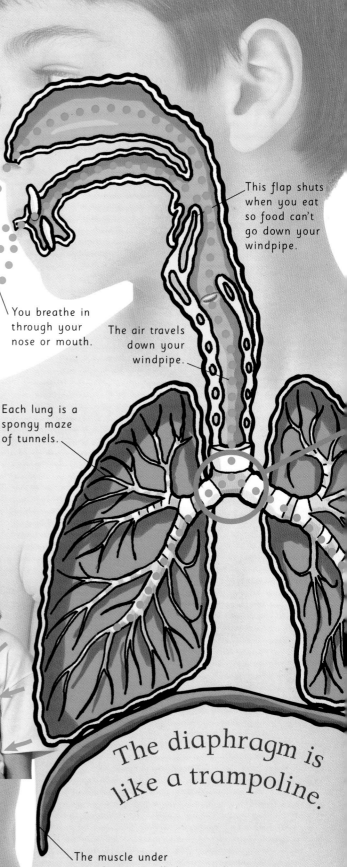

This flap shuts
when you eat
so food can't
go down your
windpipe.

You breathe in
through your
nose or mouth.

The air travels
down your
windpipe.

Each lung is a
spongy maze
of tunnels.

The diaphragm is
like a trampoline.

When you breathe
in, your lungs
stretch out and
take in lots of air.

When you
breathe out
your lungs
squash down
forcing all the
air out.

The muscle under
your lungs is called
the diaphragm. It
moves up and down
as you breathe.

In and out

Your ribs and diaphragm help you to
breathe. Your lungs fill with air when
you raise your ribcage, then empty out
when you lower it. A muscle called the
diaphragm helps you do this.

60

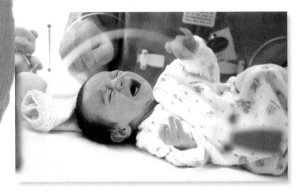

A helping hand
Some newborn babies have trouble breathing. They are put into an enclosed cradle called an incubator. Extra oxygen is pumped into the incubator for them.

The view from the bottom of your windpipe.

Windpipe
Air from your mouth and nose enters your windpipe, which goes down your throat into your chest. Then it splits into two passages – one for each lung.

The alveoli are surrounded by tiny blood capillaries to take the oxygen round the body.

Air sacs
Your lungs are full of tunnels ending in tiny air sacs called alveoli. Here, oxygen from the air passes into your blood. Your blood carries oxygen around every part of your body.

Curiosity quiz
Take a look through these images related to breathing. You should be able to find them all in the next few pages.

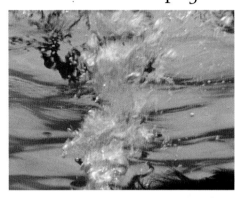

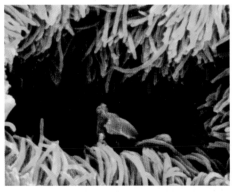

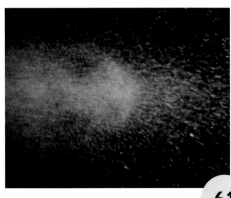

About 23,000.

Air and oxygen

The air you breathe contains a life-giving gas called oxygen. Oxygen helps your cells get their energy from food. They would die within minutes if you stopped breathing.

Oxygen

Carbon dioxide

During the day, trees take in carbon dioxide from the air and give out oxygen.

Oxygen from trees

Trees help to clean the air by filtering out pollution. They also make oxygen, which they release through their leaves.

You normally take about 20 breaths per minute – more if you're exercising.

What is in air?

Air is all around you, but you can't see, smell, or taste it. You can feel it when the wind blows.

Become an expert...

on cells, the body's building blocks, page **8-9**

Puffed out

Breathing heavily gives your body extra oxygen so it can work harder. You feel puffed out and pant when your lungs can't supply your body with oxygen quickly enough.

What is the kiss of life?

Airless places

Not every place has air to breathe, so sometimes people carry their own.

Fires burn up oxygen and produce thick, poisonous smoke.

Mountain tops have thin air with little oxygen.

Space and planets near Earth have no air to breathe.

Water contains oxygen, but humans cannot breathe it.

When you breathe out under water you make bubbles.

Hold that breath!

People can spend a few moments under water without breathing. Most people can manage about a minute, but the world record is around six minutes.

On a cold day you can see the water in your breath turn to steam as it meets the air.

Wet air

Have you noticed that when you breathe onto a window or a mirror it becomes wet? That's because the air you breathe out is slightly damp.

You need to be able to control your breathing to blow up a balloon.

How much puff have you got?

How much air?

You take in about half a litre (0.8 pints) of air with each breath. If you breathe in deeply you can take in about 3 litres (5 pints) in one gulp.

A way of helping someone who has stopped breathing by blowing into their mouth.

Making sounds

Humans can make many more
sounds than other creatures.
Because the shape of your
face affects your voice,
your voice is unique.

You can speak, whisper, hum, and shout!

Voice box

Your voice box has two jobs. You
use it to make sounds, and to seal
off your windpipe when you
eat so you don't choke.

Open vocal cords

Vocal cords

Inside your voice box are
two flaps called vocal
cords. You make sounds
by pushing air between
them, causing them to
vibrate. Fast vibrations
produce high sounds,
slower ones, low sounds.

Closed vocal cords

Adam's apple

During puberty, a
boy's voice box
grows bigger, giving
him a deeper voice.
You can sometimes
see it bulging at the
front of the throat. It
is known as the
Adam's apple.

Adam's
apple

Air supply

You use the air coming
out of your lungs to
produce sounds. So it's
difficult to speak when
you're breathless.

Why do babies and children have higher voices than adults?

Loud sounds

The harder air is forced out of the lungs, the louder the sound. So when a baby takes a big gulp of air you can expect a really big cry!

Do you know a snorer?

ZZZZZ

Shaping words

The air coming from the lungs is shaped by the tongue, cheeks, and lips to form specific sounds.

Oo is made by pursing your lips and pushing them out.

Ah sounds are made with a low tongue and a wide open mouth.

Ee is made by stretching your lips and keeping your tongue up high.

ZZZZZ

Snoring

Sometimes, when people sleep, the fleshy parts at the back of the nose and throat vibrate as they breathe. This rattling is called snoring. It can also happen when you have a cold.

Didgeridoo

Making music

You control your breath when you speak, but you need really excellent breath control to sing or play a wind instrument.

Become an expert...

on puberty, pages **102-103** on body language, pages **112-113**

They have shorter vocal cords, which vibrate faster, producing higher sounds.

Ah-choo!

You need to keep your airways clear to breathe at all times. If something gets into your airways you have to get it out pretty quickly!

A sneeze can travel as fast as a car!!!!

Sneezing

Sneezes are a quick way to get rid of unwanted particles that you have accidentally breathed into your nose.

Why do you close your eyes when you sneeze?

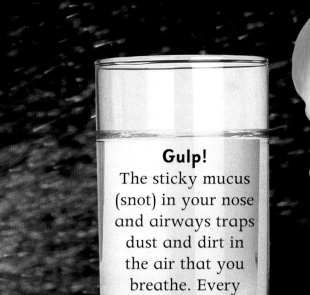

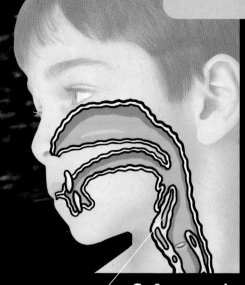

Gulp!

The sticky mucus (snot) in your nose and airways traps dust and dirt in the air that you breathe. Every day you swallow about a glass of the stuff.

Usually the flap is up, holding your windpipe open.

The flap closes when you swallow.

Safety catch

Unlike other animals, human beings use the throat both for eating and breathing. The epiglottis is a small flap of cartilage that shuts off your windpipe when you swallow so food can't accidentally go down it and choke you.

Nose hairs

The tiny hairs in your nose work like brooms to sweep out any particles that you've breathed in. They get trapped in mucus and are swept along to be swallowed down your throat.

get into it

Yawning is catching! Is there anyone nearby? Give a yawn and see if you can start a yawning epidemic!

Coughing

Irritating particles that have entered your throat are thrown out when you cough. Coughing uses your vocal cords, which is why a noise comes out with the cough.

Hiccups

Sometimes your diaphragm suddenly tightens, causing air to rush into your lungs. This makes your vocal cords snap closed with a "hic". Hiccups seem to happen for no reason.

Yawning

Nobody knows why we yawn but we do know one effect of yawning: more oxygen in the lungs. It seems we yawn to perk ourselves up when we're feeling tired or bored.

To stop your eyeballs shooting out of your face with the force of the sneeze.

All wrapped up

Skin covers your whole body. It protects you from germs, water, and sunshine, and helps keep your body at the right temperature.

The skin on your eyelids is the thinnest on your body.

Two layers

Your skin has two main layers. The top one – the one you can see – is called the epidermis. Underneath is the dermis, where there are nerves and blood vessels.

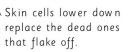

There are flat cells on the surface of your skin. These are made from a tough material called keratin. When the cells die, they dry out and flake off.

Skin cells lower down replace the dead ones that flake off.

Skin is a sort of stretchy overcoat.

Heavy load

Skin is the heaviest single part of your body. It can weigh as much as a bag of shopping.

Waterproof seal

Skin stops water getting into your body when you have a shower or go for a swim. It also stops fluids escaping from inside you.

Magnified skin flakes

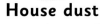

House dust

Dust is mostly made of dead skin. Dust mites feed on this skin. They live in beds, pillows, and carpets.

Dust mites aren't really this big! They're so small you can't see them.

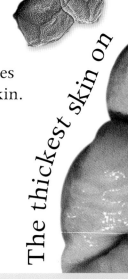

The thickest skin on

How many dead skin flakes fall off every day?

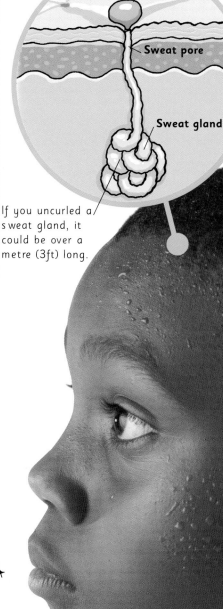

Sweat

Sweat pore

Sweat gland

If you uncurled a sweat gland, it could be over a metre (3ft) long.

Skin colour

The colour of your skin is affected by a substance called melanin. The more melanin you have, the darker you will be. When you are outside in the sun, your body produces extra melanin to protect your skin. This melanin makes your skin darker and you get a suntan.

your body is on the soles of your feet.

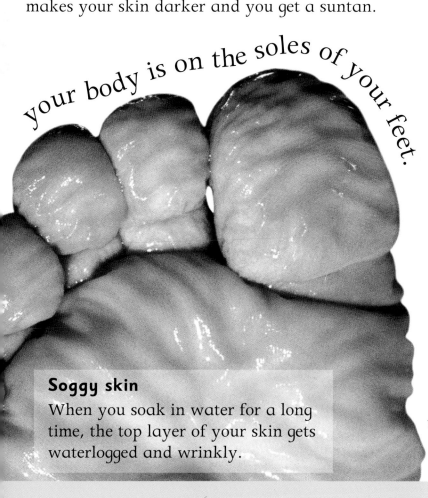

Soggy skin

When you soak in water for a long time, the top layer of your skin gets waterlogged and wrinkly.

Cooling down

When sweat dries on your skin, it helps to cool you down. Sweat comes from coiled tubes under the surface. It gets out through tiny holes called pores.

69

About ten million.

At your fingertips

Your fingertips have the most sensitive skin on your body.

Nails work with skin to protect your body. They stop you hurting the ends of your fingers and help you to pick things up.

Roll the soft part of your fingertip on an ink pad. Now roll your inky fingertip on a piece of paper. The mark you make is your very own fingerprint.

Arch

Loop

Whorl

Fingertip patterns
Fingertips are covered with swirly ridges that help you grip things. These are called fingerprints. Everyone has different fingerprints with different patterns such as arches, loops, or whorls.

The skin around your joints is loose and saggy so you can bend them easily.

On the surface
To the naked eye, your hand looks smooth and solid.

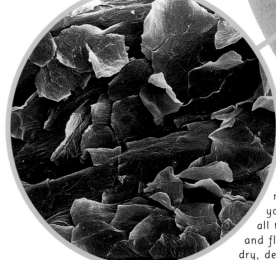

Sweat leaves almost invisible marks on all the surfaces you touch.

Police use fingerprints to help catch criminals.

Under a microscope, you can see all the folds and flakes of dry, dead skin.

Why do you get white spots on your nails?

Nails grow from a root under your cuticle.

Cuticle

Fat

Bone

When you look at nail keratin close up, it has lots of flaky layers.

The inside story

Although nails are much harder than skin or hair, they're made from the same basic material. It is called keratin.

Our nails are like animals' claws.

Family connections

Like humans, birds and animals have body parts that are made of keratin.

Claws look like nails, but they are stronger and sharper.

Beaks are very hard so birds can tear food and crack seeds.

Holding on

It would be difficult to hold heavy things if you didn't have fingernails. They help to make your fingertips straight and strong. The other reason you have fingernails is so you can scratch when you're itchy!

Nail growth

Nails start to grow before you're born, and they carry on your whole life. They grow quicker on your hands than on your feet.

Horns contain different kinds of keratin. Rhino horns are made of hair keratin.

These spots mean the new nail has been banged or knocked.

Fairly hairy

Hair is mostly made of keratin, just like skin and nails. You have about 100 thousand hairs on your head and millions more on your body.

Hair grows for up to seven years before it falls out.

Hair close up

Each hair is covered with scales that overlap like roof tiles. This makes the hair strong and protects it. Hair is dead tissue, which is why it doesn't hurt to cut it.

What's your hair like?

Hair grows out of tiny pockets or follicles. The shape of these pockets controls whether hair is straight, wavy, or curly.

Like moulds, follicles shape each strand of hair. Straight hair grows out of straight follicles.

Slightly curvy follicles produce wavy strands of hair.

Head hair

Lots of body heat escapes from your head, so the hair there is long and thick to keep your brain warm. Fine hairs cover every other part of you except the palms of your hands, soles of your feet, and your lips.

How many hairs do you lose from your head every day?

Smooth surface

Some men lose their hair as they grow older. In fact, the hair still grows, but it is shorter and falls out more easily. A few people are born without any hair at all – not even eyelashes.

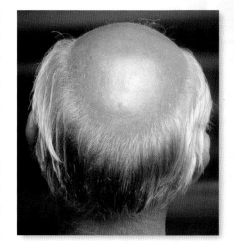

Colour chart

Hair, like skin, gets its colour from a chemical called melanin. If you have no melanin in your hair, it will be white – if you have lots, it will be jet black.

Brrrr...

When you're cold, tiny muscles pull your body hair upright so it forms a fuzzy layer to keep warmth in. When the muscles pull, they make little ridges called goose pimples.

Goose pimple

Follicles that are very swirly in shape produce tightly curled hair.

Good food

If your head is itchy, you may have head lice. These creatures cling to your hair and suck blood from your scalp. When you play with friends, the lice crawl from one head to another. These fussy bugs like clean heads best.

Germs

Your body is a walking zoo. It's covered with bugs that feed and breed on you but are mostly too small to see. Many do no harm, but some, called germs, make you ill when they get inside you.

Viruses spread through the air in coughs and sneezes.

These viruses give people colds or the flu.

Vile viruses

Viruses are the smallest living things on Earth. They break into cells and force them to make new viruses. Viruses can cause colds, flu, measles, mumps, and warts.

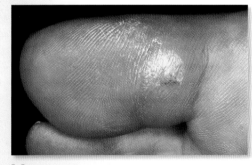

Verucca

A verruca (wart) is a patch of thickened skin caused by a virus. The virus often spreads from person to person in places where people walk barefoot, such as swimming pools.

Become an expert...

on clearing airways, pages **66-67**

visiting the doctor, pages **110-111**

What animal has killed more people than any other?

Beastly bacteria

Bacteria are very common germs that often spread by touch. When bacteria get into cuts, they cause swellings and sores. Certain types cause deadly diseases if they get into your stomach or lungs.

Your hand leaves bacteria on anything you touch

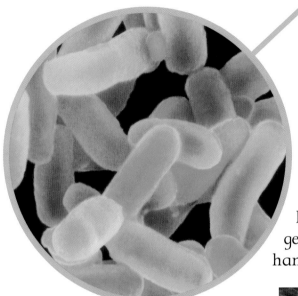

Billions of Bacteria

There are more bacteria on your skin than there are people in the world. Most do little harm, and some actually protect you from other germs. If you touch rotten food or faeces, your hands will pick up more dangerous bacteria.

Big bugs

Creatures much bigger than bacteria or viruses also feed on your body and can make you sick.

 Giardia live in intestines and spread in dirty water. They cause diarrhoea.

 Threadworms live in the large intestine and spread on dirty fingers.

 Follicle mites live in the roots of most people's eyelashes and do little harm.

 Mosquitos suck people's blood and spread germs that cause deadly diseases.

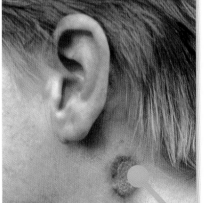

Fungi

Some germs are fungi (related to mushrooms). Tinea (ringworm) is a type of fungus that grows through skin like a plant, sending out long thin shoots.

The tinea fungus grows through your skin like a plant, sending out long thin shoots.

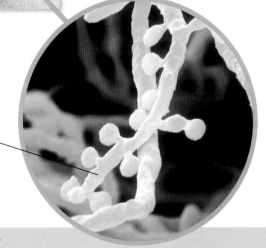

Body defences

Although you can't see them, germs are always landing on your body and trying to get inside it. Your body has lots of clever ways of keeping them out.

Poison tears

Germs that land on your eyes are washed away by tears, which come from glands above your eyes. Tears contain the chemical lysozyme, which kills bacteria by making them burst open.

You make about 1 litre (2 pints) of saliva a day.

Saved by spit

The liquid in your mouth is called saliva. As well as helping you digest food, saliva protects your mouth, tongue, and teeth from attack by bacteria.

Sticky business

Germs get into your lungs when you breathe in. They get trapped in a sticky liquid called mucus, which lines your airways. Tiny beating hairs continually push the mucus up to your throat to be swallowed.

Earwax flows slowly out of your ears all the time, flushing out dirt and germs.

Which is your largest defensive organ?

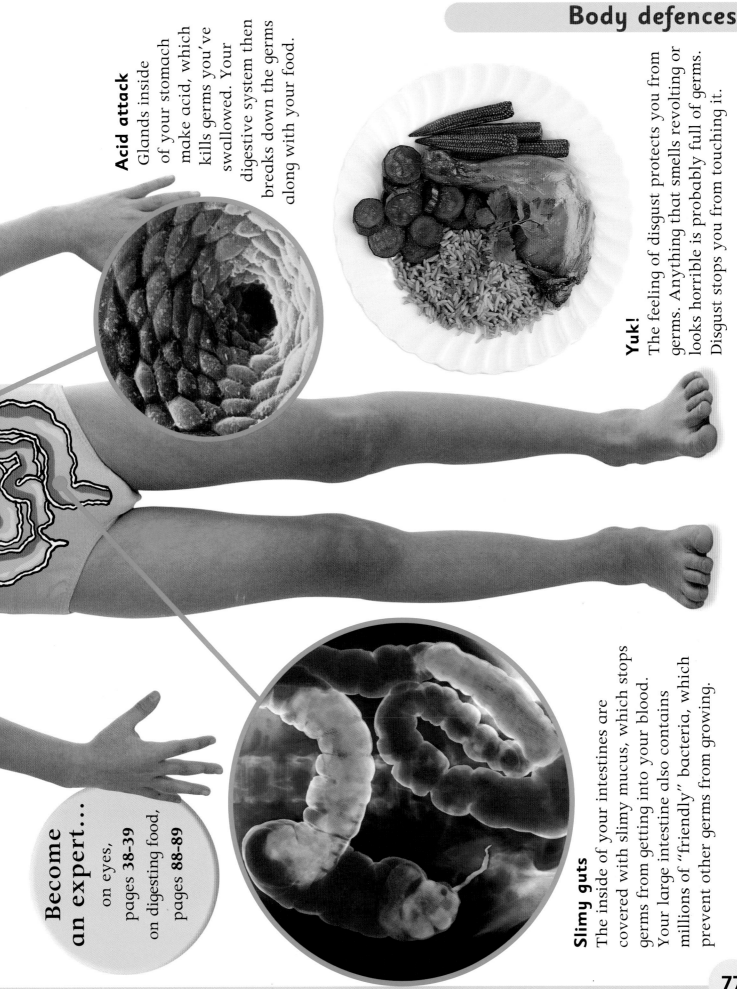

Acid attack

Glands inside of your stomach make acid, which kills germs you've swallowed. Your digestive system then breaks down the germs along with your food.

Yuk!

The feeling of disgust protects you from germs. Anything that smells revolting or looks horrible is probably full of germs. Disgust stops you from touching it.

Slimy guts

The inside of your intestines are covered with slimy mucus, which stops germs from getting into your blood. Your large intestine also contains millions of "friendly" bacteria, which prevent other germs from growing.

Become an expert...

on eyes, pages 38-39
on digesting food, pages 88-89

Your skin.

Fighting germs

If germs break through your outer defences and invade your tissues, your body fights back. The cells of your immune system hunt and destroy germs. This system also remembers germs and protects you from them in the future.

Antibodies attacking germs.

Killer cells

White blood cells called macrophages kill germs by swallowing them. When a macrophage finds a germ, it stretches out, wraps around the germ, and pulls it inside. Digestive juices then destroy it.

Antibodies

Some white blood cells make chemicals called antibodies. These stick to the surface of germs, telling other body cells to attack.

Antibody

This germ is being swallowed.

This white blood cell is called a macrophage.

Heating up
Your body gets hotter when it fights germs, which gives you a high temperature.

How many tonsils are in your throat?

Lymph system

Fluid continually leaks out of your blood vessels and tissues. It returns to the blood through tubes called lymph vessels. Dotted along these are swellings called nodes, which filter out germs.

Extra protection

Doctors protect you from germs with vaccines. Vaccines contain weak or dead germs that your immune system learns to attack. If the real germ ever gets inside you, your immune system remembers it and attacks very quickly.

Killer milk

Breast milk contains germ-killing antibodies that protect babies from disease. During the first few days of a baby's life, the mother makes a special milk called colostrum, which is packed with antibodies.

The swellings in lymph vessels are called lymph nodes.

Tonsils

At the back of your mouth are several patches of tissue called tonsils. They are full of white blood cells that fight germs in your throat. However, the tonsils sometimes fill with germs themselves and have to be removed.

Two main ones and four smaller ones.

Allergies

An allergy happens when your body mistakes a harmless substance for a germ and overreacts to it. Food, plants, dust, pets, and many other substances can cause allergies.

Allergens

A substance that triggers an allergy is called an allergen.

 Wasp stings can kill people who are allergic to them.

 Antibiotic medicines can give allergic people a rash on the skin.

 Hair and **skin** from pets can cause an allergy very similar to hayfever.

 Moulds grow in damp places. Their powdery spores can cause asthma.

 Biological washing powder can cause a skin reaction.

Who gets allergies?

If you grow up in a large family or on a farm, your immune system will get lots of practice against germs. Some experts think this makes you less likely to get allergies.

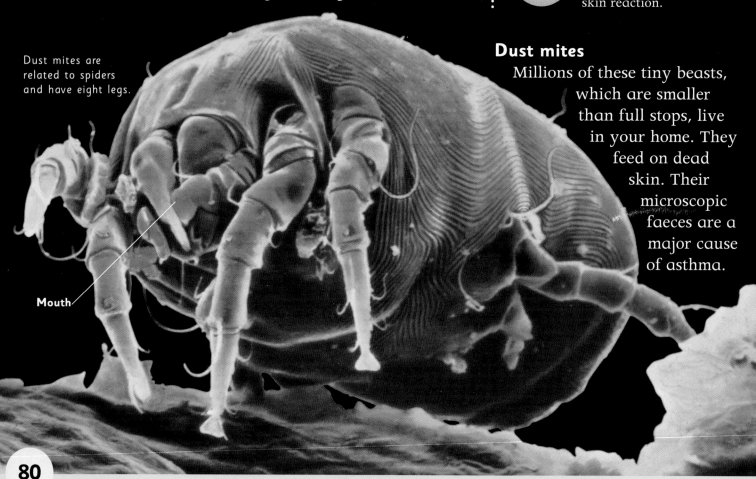

Dust mites are related to spiders and have eight legs.

Mouth

Dust mites

Millions of these tiny beasts, which are smaller than full stops, live in your home. They feed on dead skin. Their microscopic faeces are a major cause of asthma.

What's the most common type of allergy?

Poison ivy

Skin allergies

If you touch a thing you're allergic to, itchy red spots may appear on your skin. Poison ivy plants, make-up, jewellery, and clothes can cause skin allergies.

Skin allergies cause itchy red spots that can look just like a nettle rash.

Pollen

A very common cause of allergy is a powdery dust called pollen which is made by flowers. Pollen floats through the air and enters our bodies as we breathe.

Food allergies

Foods that cause allergies include strawberries, nuts, seafood, and eggs. These can give an allergic person a skin rash, a runny nose, a sore mouth, nausea, and diarrhoea.

Peanuts can be deadly to people with a nut allergy

Hayfever

People who are allergic to pollen have hayfever. When they breathe in lots of pollen, their noses run and their eyes get sore. Hayfever is worst in spring and summer, when grass flowers release lots of pollen into the air.

Hayfever can make your eyes swollen, watery, and red.

Inhalers squirt out medicine in a spray, helping people with asthma to breathe.

Asthma

People with asthma can find it hard to breathe. Their chests feel tight and their breathing becomes wheezy. Asthma can be caused by an allergy to dust mites, cat hairs, or other substances in air.

81

Hayfever.

Digestive system

Food is made up of large, complicated chemicals that your body has to break into small chemicals that your blood can absorb. This process is called digestion.

Physical digestion

Some parts of your digestive system mash up food physically, just like a food processor does. Your mouth breaks food into chunks. Your stomach then churns these around until they form a slushy liquid.

Become an expert...

on taste and smell, pages **36-37**

on what's in food, pages **106-107**

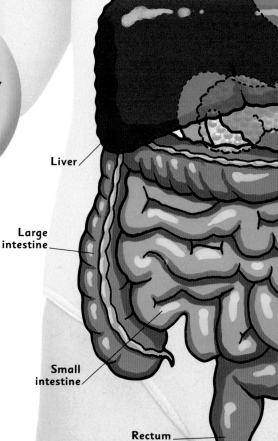

When you swallow, food passes down a tube called the oesophagus.

Tube journey

Your digestive system is really just a long, tangled tube. Food travels about 9 metres (30 feet) as it passes from start to finish.

Liver

Large intestine

Small intestine

Rectum

Venus flytrap

The Venus flytrap catches insects and digests them with enzymes.

Dragonfly

Chemical digestion

Many digestive organs make juices that break down the chemicals in food. The juices contain enzymes, which turn large food molecules into small molecules.

Which is longer: your small intestine or your large intestine?

Digesting a meal

A large meal takes a day or more to pass through your digestive system. Different digestive organs make enzymes that work on different parts of the meal.

Bread starts to break down in your mouth.

Fat starts to break down in the small intestine.

The fibre in vegetables isn't digested.

Meat starts to break down in your stomach.

6pm
Food gets swallowed 10 seconds after it enters your mouth.

10pm
A meal spends about 4 hours in the stomach, but very rich food can spend twice as long there.

3am
The meal is slowly squeezed through your small intestine, sometimes causing loud gurgling noises.

The next day
Undigested leftovers reach the end of their journey about a day after you swallowed the food.

Stomach

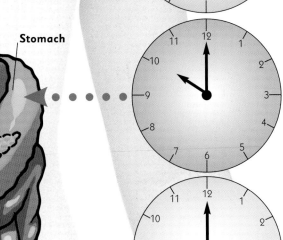

Curiosity quiz

Take a look through the digestive-system pages and see if you can spot any of the cells and tissues below.

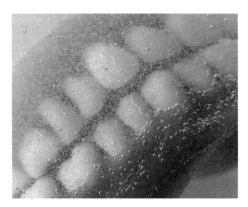

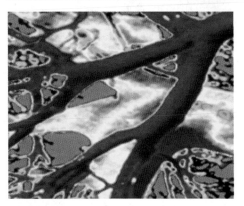

Your small intestine.

Chew it over

We use our teeth to bite off and chew our food. During the course of your life you will have two separate sets of teeth.

First teeth
Your first teeth start to grow when you're about 6 months old. The front teeth usually appear first.

Adult teeth
When you are six your first teeth start to fall out. Adult teeth with deeper roots grow to replace them.

Wisdom teeth
Your back teeth are called wisdom teeth. They appear when you are 17 or older, and sometimes not at all.

False teeth
If you don't take care of your teeth they will decay and fall out. Then you will need false teeth.

Types of teeth

Your mouth contains a selection of different types of teeth. Each type is designed to do a different job.

A child has 20 teeth, an adult has 32.

Molars at the back of your mouth have a flat edge so you can mash your food thoroughly.

Premolars roughly crush and grind your food. They are smaller than molars.

Canines grip and tear food using a single rounded point.

Incisors at the front of your mouth slice up chunks of food.

Roots

Without long roots your teeth might break or fly out of your mouth if you bit down hard on your food. The root is held in place by a kind of cement.

What is another name for your first teeth?

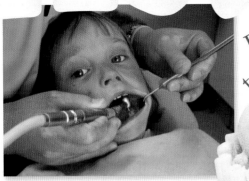

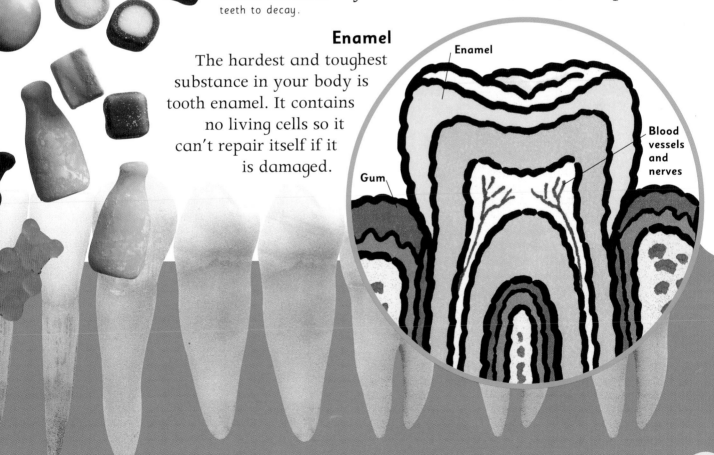

Brush twice a day to keep decay away.

Brush your teeth!

A sticky mixture of food and bacteria builds up on the surface of your teeth if you don't clean them properly. It is called plaque.

Decay

Bacteria in plaque can eat through tooth enamel and attack the blood vessels and nerves deep inside the tooth. This is called decay. It hurts, and the dentist may need to give you a filling.

The sugar in sweets sticks to your teeth, forming plaque. Plaque contains bacteria that causes teeth to decay.

Inside a tooth

Deep inside your teeth are lots of blood vessels and nerves. The nerves mean you can feel heat, cold, and pain.

Enamel

The hardest and toughest substance in your body is tooth enamel. It contains no living cells so it can't repair itself if it is damaged.

Enamel

Blood vessels and nerves

Gum

Milk teeth or baby teeth.

From mouth to stomach

You start digesting food the moment you bite into it. As your teeth tear the food apart, enzymes in your spit begin to attack it chemically. By the time it reaches your stomach, your meal is unrecognizable.

Get a grip

Your tongue is a super strong, flexible bundle of muscle that pushes food against your teeth as you chew. It has a rough surface for good grip.

Seen close up, your tongue is covered by tiny bumps and stalks that make its surface rough to improve its grip.

Mouth watering

The slimy liquid in your mouth is saliva. It moistens food to make it easier to chew and swallow. Saliva also contains an enzyme that breaks down starch, one of the main ingredients in bread, rice, and pasta.

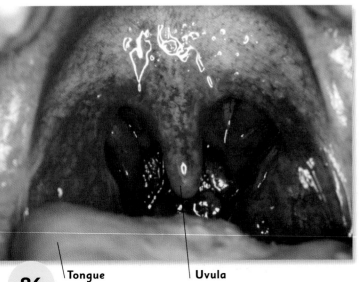

Tongue   Uvula

What is the scientific name for burping?

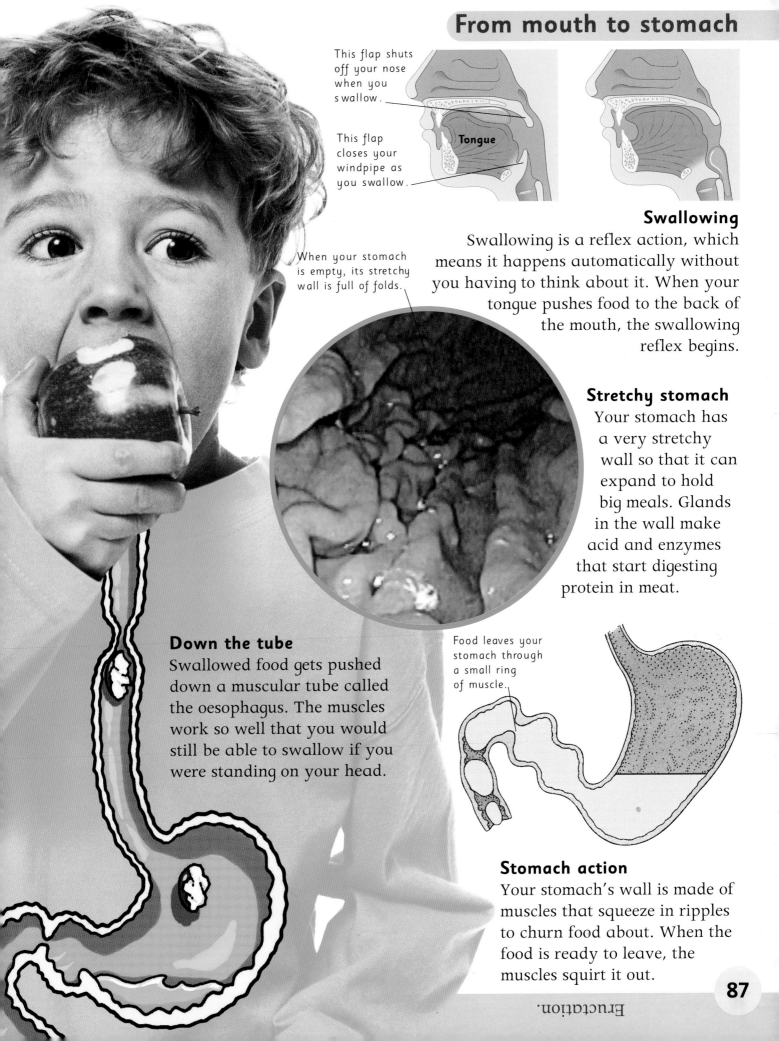

This flap shuts off your nose when you swallow.

This flap closes your windpipe as you swallow.

Tongue

When your stomach is empty, its stretchy wall is full of folds.

Swallowing

Swallowing is a reflex action, which means it happens automatically without you having to think about it. When your tongue pushes food to the back of the mouth, the swallowing reflex begins.

Stretchy stomach

Your stomach has a very stretchy wall so that it can expand to hold big meals. Glands in the wall make acid and enzymes that start digesting protein in meat.

Down the tube

Swallowed food gets pushed down a muscular tube called the oesophagus. The muscles work so well that you would still be able to swallow if you were standing on your head.

Food leaves your stomach through a small ring of muscle.

Stomach action

Your stomach's wall is made of muscles that squeeze in ripples to churn food about. When the food is ready to leave, the muscles squirt it out.

Inside the intestines

When food leaves your stomach, it enters a long, tangled tube. This has two parts. The first is your small intestine, which is long and narrow. The second is your large intestine, which is shorter but fatter.

Small intestine

The small intestine finishes off the job of digestion. Digested food soaks through its wall and enters the blood to be carried away.

Finger blobs

Tiny, finger-shaped blobs called villi line the small intestine. They speed up the absorption of food.

Muscles push food through your intestines just like this hand pushes a ball along a stocking.

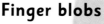

A squeezing action travels along the intestine in waves.

Pushed along

Your intestines use a special kind of muscle action called peristalsis to move food along. Rings of muscle in the intestines squeeze behind the food, pushing it.

How tall would you be if your intestines weren't coiled up?

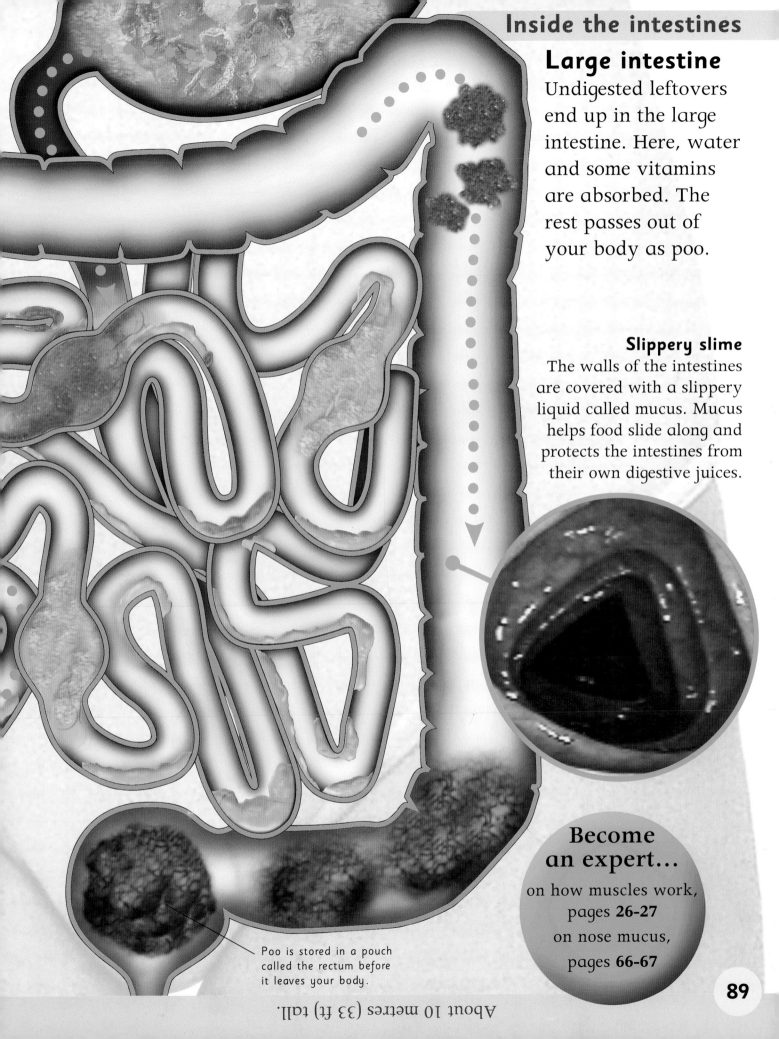

Large intestine

Undigested leftovers end up in the large intestine. Here, water and some vitamins are absorbed. The rest passes out of your body as poo.

Slippery slime

The walls of the intestines are covered with a slippery liquid called mucus. Mucus helps food slide along and protects the intestines from their own digestive juices.

Become an expert...

on how muscles work, pages **26-27**

on nose mucus, pages **66-67**

Poo is stored in a pouch called the rectum before it leaves your body.

About 10 metres (33 ft) tall.

89

Waterworks

Your body gets rid of waste chemicals and excess water by making urine. Urine comes from two organs called kidneys. They filter and clean blood as it flows through, removing chemicals that your body doesn't need.

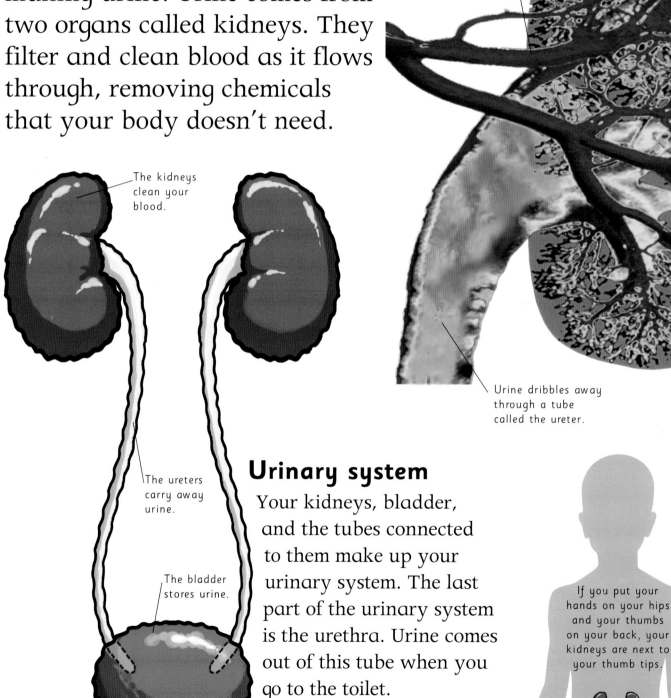

Blood flows in and out of the kidneys through large blood vessels.

The kidneys clean your blood.

Urine dribbles away through a tube called the ureter.

The ureters carry away urine.

The bladder stores urine.

Urinary system

Your kidneys, bladder, and the tubes connected to them make up your urinary system. The last part of the urinary system is the urethra. Urine comes out of this tube when you go to the toilet.

If you put your hands on your hips and your thumbs on your back, your kidneys are next to your thumb tips.

The urethra gets rid of urine.

How long do your kidneys take to clean all the blood in your body?

Inside a kidney

The blood vessels entering your kidneys divide into smaller and smaller branches. These lead to a million tiny filtering units called nephrons.

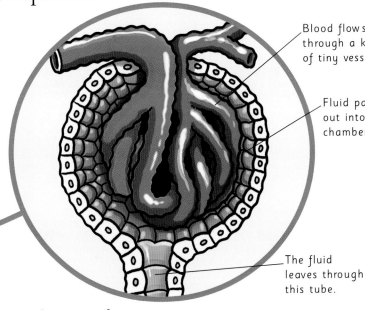

Blood flows through a knot of tiny vessels.

Fluid passes out into a chamber.

The fluid leaves through this tube.

Inside a nephron

As blood flows through a nephron, fluids leave the blood vessel and pass to a long, looped tube. Useful chemicals are then reabsorbed into blood.

Water disposal

Here's how your body gets rid of water.

 Urine makes up more than half of the water that leaves your body.

 Breath contains over a quarter of the water your body gets rid of.

 Sweat is only about one twelfth of the water leaving your body.

 Poo is fairly dry and contains only a little bit of your liquid waste.

Balancing act

Your kidneys keep the water level in your body perfectly balanced. If you drink too much, your kidneys make watery urine to get rid of any excess. When your body is short of water, your kidneys pass less into your urine.

When the water level is low, the pituitary gland releases the hormone ADH.

This part of the brain monitors the water level in blood.

A low water level also triggers a feeling of thirst, making you drink.

ADH travels to your kidneys in your blood.

Water control

Your kidneys work together with your brain to control your water level. When this level is low, your brain releases a hormone that makes your kidneys save water.

Your kidneys save water, making your urine stronger.

91

The stretchy bladder

All day long, a small stream of urine trickles out of each kidney. It collects in an organ called the bladder, which stores the urine until you go to the toilet.

Nappy rash
Babies sometimes get a rash under nappies. This happens when urine mixes with poo and makes the skin sore.

Filling up
Your bladder stretches as it fills up. This sends a signal to your brain, making you want to go to the toilet.

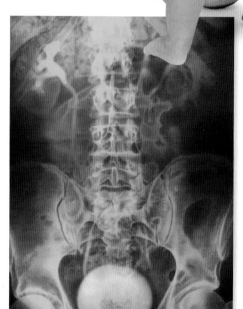

X-ray of full bladder

X-ray of empty bladder

Full stretch
An adult's bladder stretches from the size of a plum to the size of a grapefruit and can hold about 500 ml (1 pint) of urine. Your bladder is about the size of an orange when it's full.

The bladder's muscly wall squeezes to push urine out.

Inside the bladder
The bladder has a waterproof lining to stop it leaking. Urine leaves through a tube called the urethra, which is normally kept shut by two muscles.

Grapefruit   Orange

Plum

How much urine do you make each day?

What is urine?

Urine is made of water and waste chemicals. The main waste is urea, which your body makes when it breaks down protein. The colour of urine depends on how much you drink. If you drink lots of water, your urine will turn pale.

The yellow colour comes from a chemical that is made when old blood cells are broken down.

Tubes called ureters bring urine from the kidneys.

This muscle opens automatically when the bladder is full.

Urethra

We have to learn to control this muscle.

Camel urine

Camels can last for months without water so they can survive in the driest deserts. They save water by making thick, syrupy urine that is twice as salty as seawater.

Camels store fat in their humps, which they use for energy.

Bladder control

In young children, the muscles that open the bladder work automatically. As children get older, they learn to control one of the muscles.

Potty training

Children gradually gain control of their bladder around the age of two, but they still wet the bed at night. By the age of four, most children can stay dry at night as well.

Toddlers have to learn bladder control.

4–8 cupfuls, depending on how much you drink and sweat.

Making a baby

You need a mother and a father to make a baby. The mother's body does most of the work, but the father also has an important job – his sperm joins with the mother's egg and a new life begins...

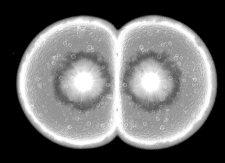

The first cells
After 36 hours, the cell has divided and made an exact copy of itself. These are the first two cells of a baby.

Eggs are the biggest cells in the human body. But they are still very small – ten would fit across a pinhead.

Sperm are amazing viewed under a microscope. They look like tiny tadpoles. You can see their tails wriggling as they swim.

Sperm race
Millions of sperm swim towards the egg cell. Only one sperm can join with the egg to make a new cell.

By the time the baby is born, the fertilized cell will have become 100 trillion cells.

What is another name for the uterus?

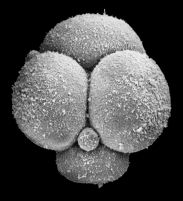

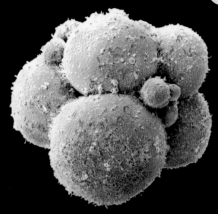

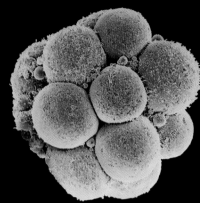

Divide again
You don't grow much in the first few days. The two cells divide to make four, then eight, and so on.

The future you
Each cell is unique to you. Cells are full of instructions about what you will look like.

At three days
The cells have carried on dividing. There are now 16 cells and they are almost ready to plant themselves in the uterus.

Where it all happens
The sperm fertilizes the egg in a tunnel, called a Fallopian tube. The fertilized egg moves down the tunnel towards the mother's uterus. The journey takes about five days.

The cells start dividing as they move down the Fallopian tube towards the uterus.

Millions of sperm from the father travel up here towards the egg.

This is the mother's ovary. It releases one egg every month.

This is the uterus. It is about the size of a pear and has muscular walls.

Arriving in the uterus
The ball of cells plants itself in the wall of the uterus. In this warm, dark place the baby will spend the next 40 weeks growing and developing.

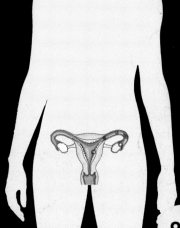

Growing in the womb

By eight weeks old, the baby is no longer a bundle of cells. It looks like a tiny person and is called a "foetus". The foetus does not eat, drink, or breathe by itself. All its needs are taken care of by its mother.

Boy or girl?

Parents can find out about a baby's health and sex before it is born. A scanning machine shows the baby on a screen. This is many parents' first sight of their child.

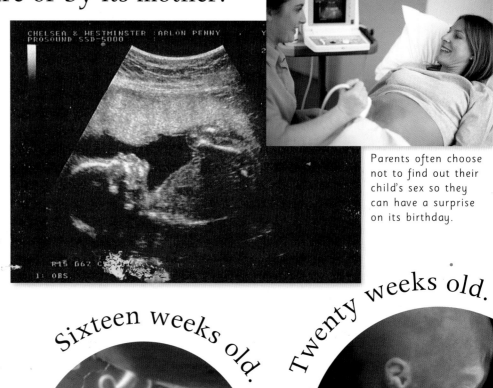

Parents often choose not to find out their child's sex so they can have a surprise on its birthday.

Eight weeks old.

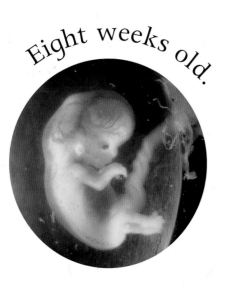

Sixteen weeks old.

Food and oxygen from the mother travel through this special cord.

Twenty weeks old.

The size of a strawberry
The foetus has eyes, a nose, lips, and a tongue. It lives in a protective bag of liquid and uses its tiny muscles to swim around gracefully.

The size of a lemon
At 16 weeks the foetus can make different faces, clench its fist, and suck its thumb. It can hear its first sounds but its eyes are not open yet.

The size of a grapefruit
At 20 weeks the foetus is getting more active. It is still quite small so there's plenty of room to kick around and turn somersaults.

When do we first start to dream?

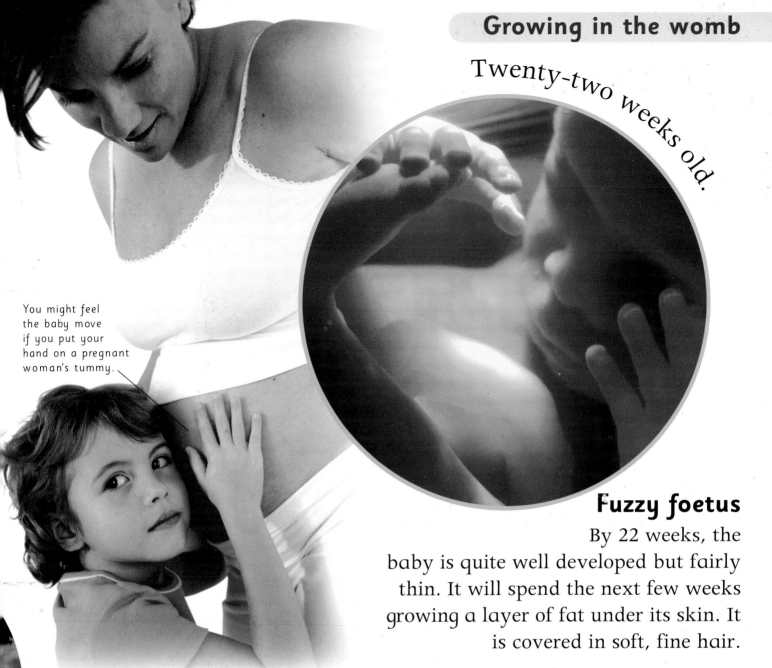

Twenty-two weeks old.

You might feel the baby move if you put your hand on a pregnant woman's tummy.

Fuzzy foetus

By 22 weeks, the baby is quite well developed but fairly thin. It will spend the next few weeks growing a layer of fat under its skin. It is covered in soft, fine hair.

What's it like in there?

It is quite noisy in the womb with the sounds of the mother's heartbeat and stomach rumbles. The baby can also hear noises outside the womb and loud bangs may make it jump. It learns to recognize its mother's voice long before it is born.

Happy birthday!

At last, after around 40 weeks, the moment comes for the baby to be born. Newborn babies can breathe, suck, and swallow. They communicate by crying if they are hungry or feel uncomfortable.

97

Before we are born, at about 20 weeks.

Identical twins

Identical twins are made when a fertilized egg splits into two separate cell clusters.

Fertilization occurs when a single sperm fuses with the egg.

The fertilized egg splits into two. We don't know what makes this happen.

Two cell clusters develop into two separate babies.

Non-identical twins

Non-identical twins are made when the mother releases two eggs instead of one.

Each egg is fertilized by a different sperm. Two babies then develop.

Growing up
Identical twins often notice amazing similarities in their taste and behaviour. Sometimes they can even tell what the other is thinking!

Double trouble

There are two different types of twins – identical and non-identical. Identical twins have the same genes. Non-identical twins are like any other brother or sister so only half their genes are the same.

Nice and cosy
The two babies grow and develop together, sharing their mother's womb. Identical twins share one placenta. Non-identical twins have a placenta each.

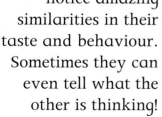

Do identical twins have exactly the same fingerprints?

Multiple births

Even rarer than being a twin is being a triplet, or even a quadruplet...

Triplets: One in 8,100 natural pregnancies produces triplets.

Quadruplets: It's rarer to be a quad. One in 729,000 pregnancies produces quads.

Quintuplets: Having five children is usually a result of fertility treatment.

Sextuplets: There are currently only around 30 sets of six in the world.

Twins in the family

Once a couple has had one set of twins, they are more likely to have another. Also, if your mother, or *her* mother, is a non-identical twin you may inherit the trait and have twins yourself!

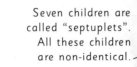

Mirror twins

Some identical twins are called mirror twins. Often, one will be left handed and the other right handed, and their fingerprints appear to mirror each other.

Seven children are called "septuplets". All these children are non-identical.

Record-breakers!

There are presently only two sets of septuplets in the world. These ones are named Kenneth, Brandon, Nathan, Joel, Alexis, Natalie, and Kelsey. They were born in Iowa in America in 1997.

No, because the soft skin on their fingertips was moulded differently in the womb.

The early years

Babies' bodies grow very fast, but their brains develop quickly too. Learning to move around and talk are both huge tasks.

Big head

Babies have enormous heads in relation to the size of their bodies! As you get older, the rest of your body catches up.

Babies' big heads hold big brains! They need them because there's lots to learn.

New skills

Children's brains are changing all the time as they learn new skills at an amazing rate.

 Smiling: most babies start to smile at around 6 weeks old.

 Drinking: babies learn to drink from a lidded cup between 6 and 12 months.

 Eating: most babies can feed themselves from a bowl at around 15 months.

 Learning colours: children can name colours by 3 years old.

 Brushing teeth: 5 year olds can brush their teeth without help.

Your body grows very fast during your first year...

Babies are so bendy they can suck their own toes!

Four days

Newborns spend most of their time asleep. Even when they're awake they don't open their eyes much.

Six weeks

Babies cry when they are cold or hungry. By this age, they start to make cooing sounds too.

Six months

Babies have a lot more control over their bodies now. Their muscles are stronger so they can sit up without help.

When do you reach half your adult height?

Chatterbox
By one year, a baby is trying to speak. By two, children can use 100 different words, and by three most know more than 1000 different words.

Being able to talk makes it easier to play with other children.

...and hardly slows down during your second!

By three, children know the difference between boys and girls.

Two years
Children this age can walk and run, climb stairs, and kick balls. They are starting to get dressed alone but can't do up buttons, zips, buckles, and shoelaces.

One year
By this age babies can understand simple words. They also take their first few steps.

101

At around two years old.

Growing up

As a child, you learn to walk and talk, run and jump, go to the toilet alone, eat with cutlery, read and write, and even make friends!

Making friends

By five years old, children can form friendships and play together. They start to care what other people think of them.

What can you do?

Do you realize how much work goes into learning all these amazing skills?

Shoelaces: At six years old, most children can do up their own shoelaces.

Riding a bike: At seven, many children can ride a two-wheeled bike.

Reading: Some children learn to read at four, some at five, and some at six!

Writing: You should write fairly clearly by the time you are seven.

As your baby fat melts away, your features become clearer...

You're learning new skills such as skipping.

Sitting still and thinking are skills too.

There's still plenty of time to play after school hours.

Age 4-5

By this age, a child can speak clearly in basic sentences, and knows many thousands of words.

Age 5-6

It's time to learn to read, write, do sums, and maybe even start playing a musical instrument.

Age 7-10

Boys and girls like different things at this age so they have more friends of their own sex.

Why do you grow?

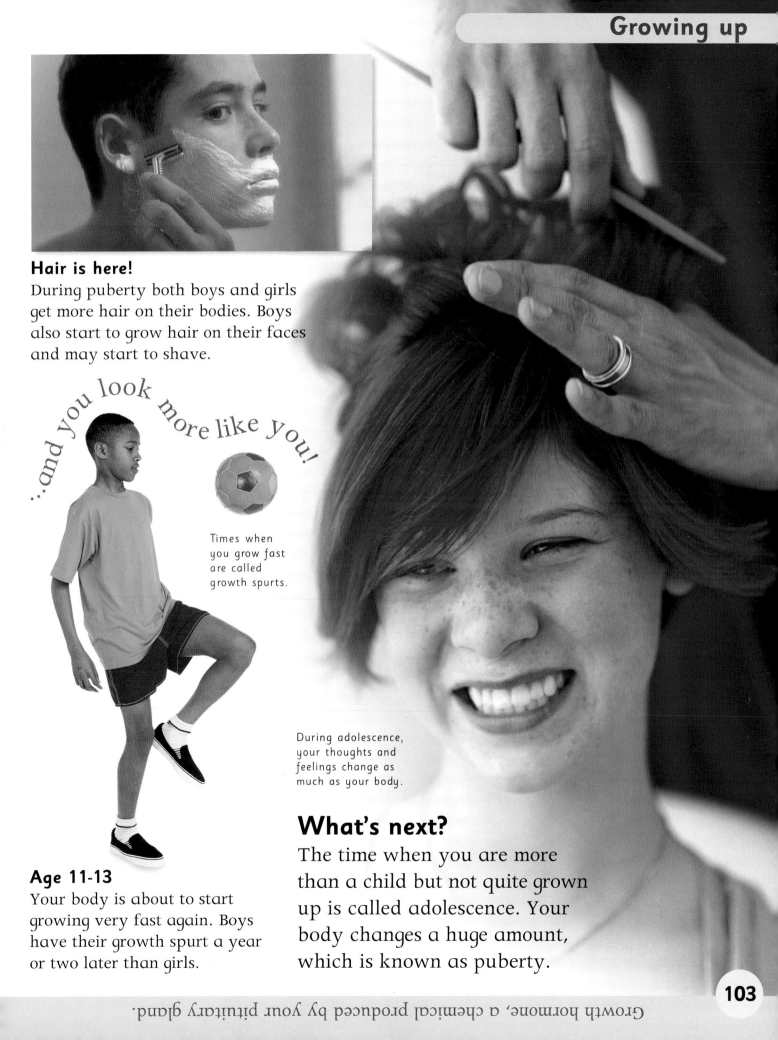

Hair is here!

During puberty both boys and girls get more hair on their bodies. Boys also start to grow hair on their faces and may start to shave.

...and you look more like you!

Times when you grow fast are called growth spurts.

During adolescence, your thoughts and feelings change as much as your body.

Age 11-13

Your body is about to start growing very fast again. Boys have their growth spurt a year or two later than girls.

What's next?

The time when you are more than a child but not quite grown up is called adolescence. Your body changes a huge amount, which is known as puberty.

103

Growth hormone, a chemical produced by your pituitary gland.

Growing older

Adults keep growing, but more slowly than children. When you get older, your body takes longer to repair itself and replace worn-out cells.

Life expectancy

As a general rule, the bigger a creature is, the longer it lives. So how long do humans live?

Butterflies have very short lives. Many live for only a month or two.

Cats kept as pets live longer than wild ones – up to 15 years.

People can live for 100 years. Women generally live longer than men.

Tortoises can live for 150 years. Some spend a quarter of their lives asleep.

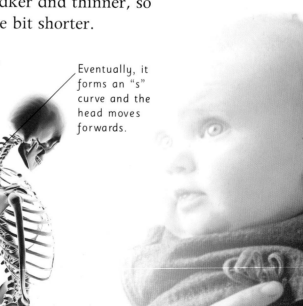

Twenties

During your twenties you are at your peak. Your body has reached its adult size so you don't spend most of your energy on growing.

Thirties

Because they're not growing any more, many people need to eat less so they don't get fat. Most bodies are strong and healthy, but athletes are already past their best.

Brittle bones

With old age, the bones and disks in the spine get weaker and thinner, so people get a little bit shorter.

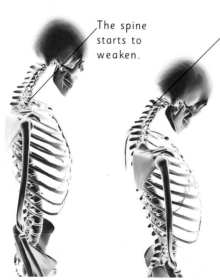

A normal, healthy spine holds the body straight.

The spine starts to weaken.

Eventually, it forms an "s" curve and the head moves forwards.

What is the longest a person has ever lived?

Smile lines

With age, skin gets less stretchy and will not smooth out when you relax your face. This is gives you wrinkles. Many cultures respect wrinkles as signs of wisdom and experience.

Silver surfer

Today people live longer than ever thanks to advances in medicine. A healthy diet, exercise, and a young mind can make old age a happy time.

Middle age

Organs and muscles are starting to get weaker. Skin on the face gets wrinkly, and hair starts to go grey. Women stop having babies.

Old age

Papery skin, weak bones, stiff joints, and bad eyesight are common in old people. Most of the organs including the lungs and heart don't work as well as they used to.

As you get older, your hair contains less melanin — the substance that gives it its colour.

Records prove that a French woman, Jeanne-Louise Calment, lived for 122 years.

What's in food?

People eat to get energy. You need a variety of foods to keep your body in peak working condition.

A balanced diet means eating everything your body needs.

Proteins
Meat, fish, eggs, beans, and nuts contain protein. Your body needs protein to repair its cells.

Carbohydrates
Bread, cereal, pasta, and sweet foods are mostly carbohydrates. You need them to give you energy.

Fat
Nuts and dairy foods, such as butter and cheese contain fat. You only need small amounts of fat.

Takeaways and fizzy drinks are nice as a treat but no substitute for a good meal.

Eat your greens
Fresh fruit and vegetables are crammed with vitamins and minerals. Your body needs these to stay healthy.

Junk food
Fast foods like hamburgers and chips contain unhealthy amounts of fat and salt, and few vitamins.

What is a vegetarian?

Water

Your body is two thirds water, but you're losing water all the time. You could live for several weeks without food but only for about 3 days without water.

You need about six glasses of liquid every day but some of this can come from your food.

Allergies

If your body reacts badly to a certain food and makes you ill, you may be allergic to it.

Wheat isn't good for some people. They cannot eat normal bread.

Nuts can be dangerous – even in tiny quantities – if you have a nut allergy.

Cows' milk doesn't suit some people, but they can drink sheep or goats' milk.

Sunshine food

You need vitamin D for strong bones. It is found in fish and eggs, but your body can produce it when you get sunlight on your skin.

Food gives you energy.

Become an expert...

on chewing food, pages **86-87**
on making urine, pages **90-91**

Fuel for your body

An orange gives you enough energy to cycle for 5 minutes. A chocolate bar gives you enough energy to cycle for 45 minutes.

The amount of energy you get from food is measured in calories.

A person who does not eat meat.

Sleep

When you sleep your body rests.
Your brain stops dealing with things
in the outside world, and uses this
time to sort out the events of the day.

Adults need
about seven
hours sleep.

A three
year old
needs about
12 hours sleep.

A newborn baby can
sleep for 20 hours a day.
By six months, 15 hours
is usually enough.

How much sleep?

As we grow older we
need less sleep. Young
adults need about eight
hours, while over 60s
may need only six.

Sleep patterns

Throughout the night,
you move in and out of
shallow and deep sleep
several times. As the hours
pass, sleep gradually
becomes lighter until
you wake up.

Time for bed.

Awake

The yellow dots show

Shallow sleep

9   10   11   12   1

Deep sleep

108

What is insomnia?

Dreaming

Everyone dreams. When you dream, your eyelids flicker. This is called rapid eye movement, or REM, sleep.

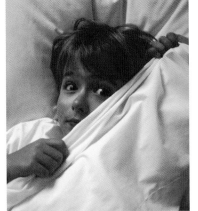

Nightmares

Nightmares are scary dreams that can wake you up and make you feel frightened or sad. During nightmares, people often think they are being chased or bullied.

When you dream, anything is... possible!

Everyone dreams, but not everyone remembers their dreams.

What dreams mean

People are fascinated by what dreams mean. We don't know for sure but...

Flying can mean that you feel powerful and free of problems.

Being naked sometimes means you are afraid of being weak.

Falling may mean you feel out of control or are scared of losing something.

when you dream.

2 3 4 5 6

Good morning!

Sleep walking

During deep sleep, parts of the brain stay awake. People may talk, or get up and walk around. They usually don't remember they have done this.

The medical name for being unable to fall or stay asleep.

Doctors and dentists

When you are ill you visit the doctor. First, the doctor examines you. Next, the doctor prescribes treatment or medicine to make you better.

The examination

The doctor asks you about your symptoms and then looks at and listens to different parts of your body.

Ears, nose, and throat

Doctors use an otoscope to examine your ears, nose, and throat. Swelling or itchiness may mean you have an infection.

Say "ah"

The doctor uses a stick to hold your tongue down and look at your tonsils. If your tonsils often get infected you may need an operation to remove them.

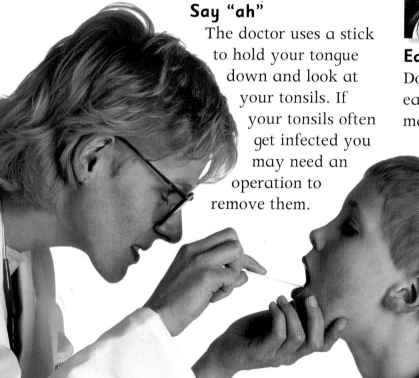

It is your tonsils' job to stop germs getting down your throat.

Hear, hear

Doctors use an instrument called a stethoscope to listen to your heartbeat or to hear how well your lungs are working.

What is a paediatrician?

Tools of the trade

Doctors keep a few simple instruments in their surgeries to help them examine their patients.

A stethoscope allows the doctor to listen to your heart or your breathing.

A rubber hammer is banged against your knee to test your reflexes.

An ophthalmoscope has a bright light for looking at the back of your eyes.

Syringes are used to give people injections to stop them getting some diseases.

Medicine comes from a pharmacy. The doctor just gives you a prescription.

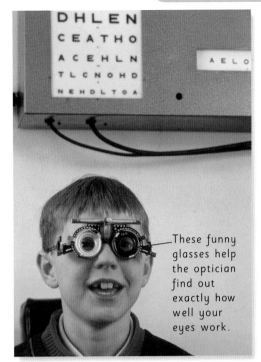

These funny glasses help the optician find out exactly how well your eyes work.

Eye spy

Opticians test your sight and work out whether you need glasses. They test each eye separately because often one can see better than the other. Your eyesight changes so you need to get your eyes tested every year.

Open wide

You can look after your teeth by brushing them, but you should still get them checked twice a year by a dentist. Hopefully, you won't need any fillings.

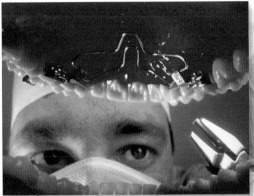

Brace yourself

Orthodontists are dentists who straighten out crooked teeth. They do this by fitting your mouth with braces to push your teeth gradually into the right position.

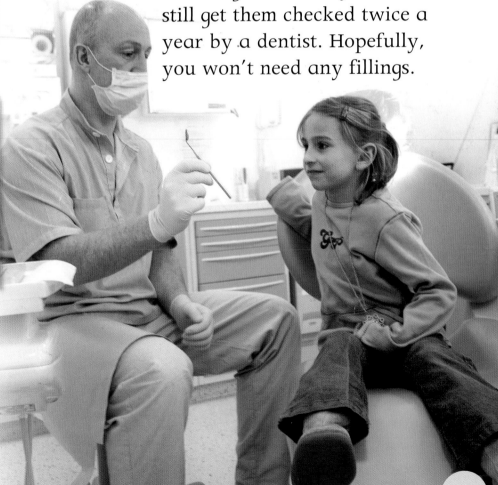

A doctor who specializes in children's illnesses.

Body language

You don't just talk with words – you also use your hands, face, and body. The look on your face and the way you stand can say a lot about how you really feel.

Personal space

People show how well they know each other by how close they stand or how often they touch. It's rude to stand too close to a stranger but normal to stand close to a best friend.

Only best friends and family can enter the **close intimate zone**.

The **intimate zone** is where people who know you well can stand while talking to you.

The **personal zone** is for people who know you but aren't close, such as teachers.

The **social zone** is where strangers stand while talking to you.

These girls are copying each other's body language.

Copying

Good friends often mimic each other's body language without realizing. They might walk in step, sit or stand in the same position, or copy each other's hand movements.

Who's in charge?

One of the things people signal with their body is whether they're in charge or somebody else is in charge. Leaning forwards or looking relaxed are ways of appearing to be in charge.

This boy's relaxed posture shows he feels very confident.

How does a dog show it knows you're in charge?

Learning gestures

You pick up a lot of your body language from the people you grow up with. Your gestures and the way you sit, stand, and walk are probably similar to your friends and family.

Open or closed?

When someone feels relaxed or friendly, they have an "open" posture, with arms and legs apart. If someone is nervous or awkward, they have a "closed" posture, with arms and legs close to the body.

Boys often learn their gestures from older brothers, and girls pick up many of theirs from older sisters.

Talking to animals

Animals can't understand speech but they often understand our body language. Dogs can sense who's in charge from body language. They need to be treated strictly or will start to misbehave.

Become an expert...

on muscles and movement, pages **26-27**

It lowers its body and tail and flattens its ears.

Use your hands

Most people move their hands as they speak, but what do their gestures mean? Some hand gestures mean the same thing all over the world, but others vary from place to place.

Speak to the hands

Hands seem to have minds of their own. When people talk, their hands move all over the place, even when they're on the phone!

Thumbs up

A raised thumb means "good" or "well done!" in North America. In Germany it means "one", in Japan it means "five", and in the Middle East and Africa it's impolite.

Making a circle

A finger touching a thumb means "OK" in North America, "worthless" in France, and "I want my change in coins" in Japan. In Turkey it can be rude.

Palms together

This is a sign of prayer in Christian countries, but in India it is used as a greeting. Indians place their hands together, make a slight bow, and say *Namaste*.

Shaking hands

Shaking hands is a common greeting in many countries, but there are slight differences. A firm handshake is a sign of sincerity in Europe but is thought to be aggressive in Asia.

In some countries, women never shake hands with men.

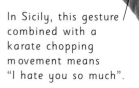

In Sicily, this gesture combined with a karate chopping movement means "I hate you so much".

How does a diver say "shark" underwater?

Pointing with an outstretched arm means something is far away.

Making a point

Pointing is one of the first hand gestures that people learn, and it means the same thing all over the world. Babies ask for things by pointing at them before they learn to speak.

Become an expert... on the bones in your hands, page **20-21**

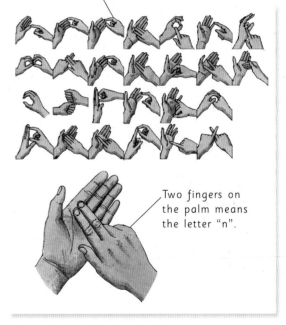

These 26 signs stand for the letters of the alphabet in British sign language.

Two fingers on the palm means the letter "n".

Talking underwater

Divers can't speak underwater so they use a kind of sign language instead. They have special signs for marine animals like sharks and turtles.

OK is shown by a finger touching a thumb, making a circle.

Stay at this depth is shown by waving a flat hand from side to side.

Stop is shown by a clenched fist and a bent arm.

Sign language

Deaf people communicate without hearing by reading lips, using facial expressions, or using sign language. Sign language varies a lot from country to country.

By making a shark's fin on the head with one hand.

Express yourself

Your face helps you communicate by showing how you feel. All over the world, people use the same facial expressions to show the six main emotions.

2 Surprised
When you're surprised, your eyebrows shoot up, your eyes open wide, and your jaw drops. Some people clap the side of their face or cover their mouth as well.

Surprise makes you gasp for breath because the hormone adrenaline makes your lungs work faster.

1 Happy
In a genuine smile, the eyes crease and the cheeks rise. A smile means the same thing whether you live in the Sahara desert or Amazon rainforest.

Grumpy or angry people sometimes look red around the eyes.

3 Angry
An angry person's eyebrows move down, their eyes narrow, and their mouth closes tightly. They might also glare without blinking.

How many facial expression are there?

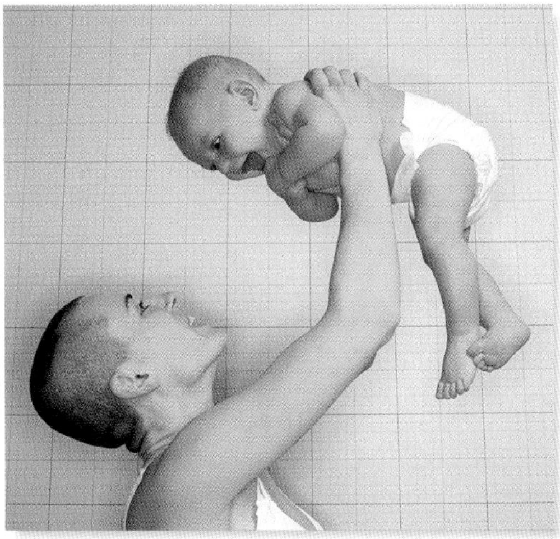

Baby face

Babies communicate with their faces before they learn to talk. They smile, frown, and show all the main emotions.

Babies learn to mirror their parents' smiles from a very early age.

Become an expert...
on how babies develop, pages **100-101**

5 Afraid
Fear raises the eyelids, making the eyes look white. The mouth opens wide in horror, and blood may drain from the face, making the skin pale.

4 Sad
In an unhappy face, the mouth droops, the inner ends of the eyebrows go up, and wrinkles appear above the nose. Powerful feelings of sadness also make people cry.

6 Disgusted
Wrinkles across the nose and narrow eyes are signs of disgust. The sight of disgust in someone's face can make you feel disgusted too.

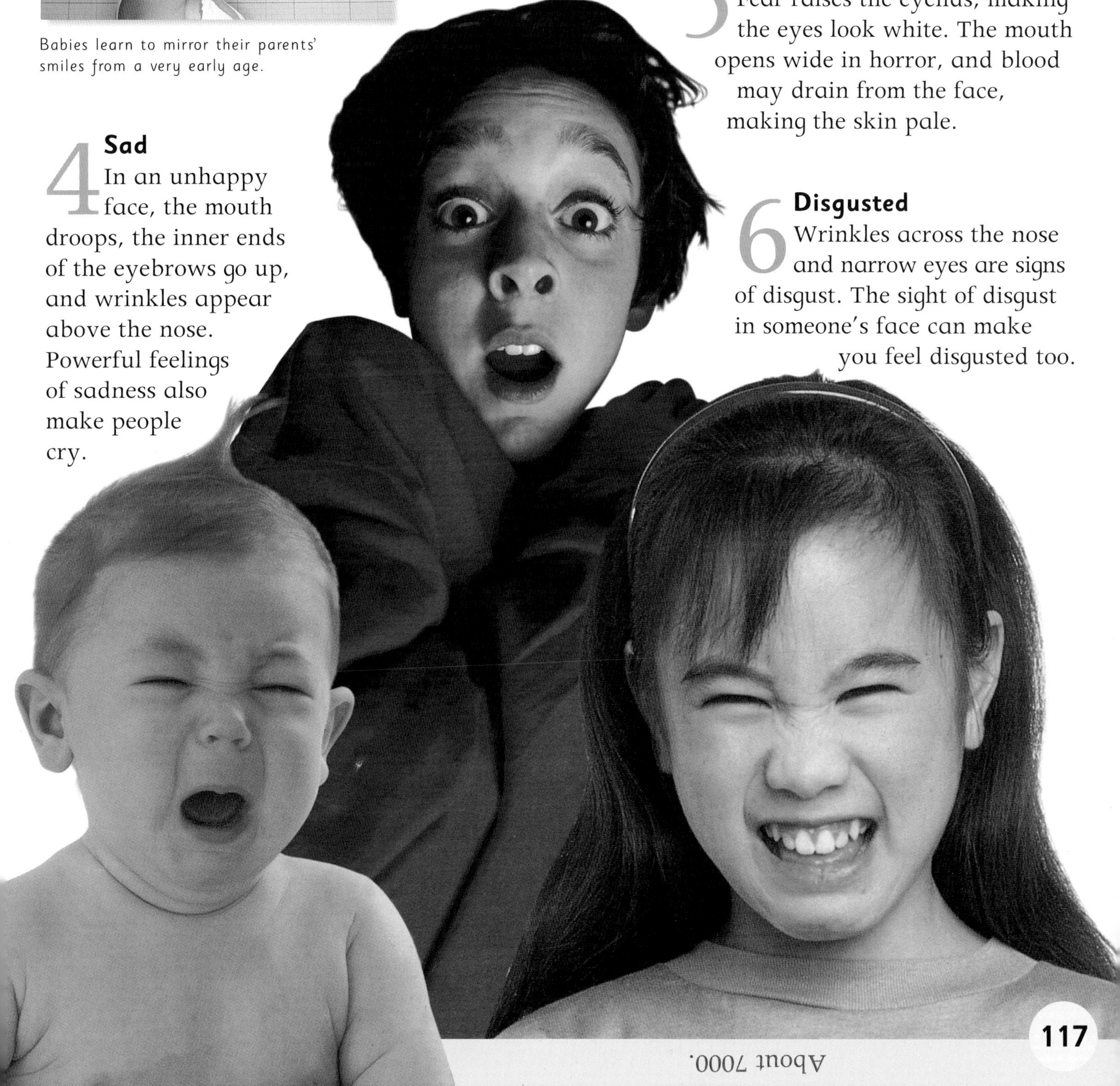

117

About 7000.

Amazing facts about YOU!

Skeleton and bones

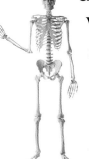

Without a skeleton to hold you up, you'd collapse on the ground like a heap of jelly.

 Your smallest bone is the stapes in your ear, which is smaller than a rice grain.

 Weight for weight, bones are stronger than steel or concrete.

 A baby has more than 300 bones but adults have only 206.

Muscles and movement

Muscles move your body by pulling bones. You use hundreds of them when you walk.

Every hair in your body has a tiny muscle that can pull it upright.

Your strongest muscle is the masseter (jaw muscle), which closes your mouth.

You use more muscles when you frown than when you smile.

Brain and nerves

Your brain is the body's control centre. Signals zoom to and from the brain along your nerves.

 Nerves carry signals at up to 400 kph (250 mph).

 Your brain is made of about 100 billion tiny cells called neurons.

 The left side of your brain controls the right side of your body and vice versa.

 The human eye can see a candle flame at night from 1.6 km (1 mile) away.

 When you're bored, the pupils in your eyes get smaller.

Heart and blood

Your heart pumps blood around your body. It works nonstop without getting tired.

 Your smallest blood vessels are ten times thinner than a hair.

 Your body contains enough blood vessels to circle the world twice.

Breathing

Lungs take air into your body so that life-giving oxygen can enter your blood.

 Laid out, the inside of your lungs is a third as big as a tennis court.

 The fastest recorded sneeze reached 167 kph (104 mph).

 In one day you breathe in enough air to fill 33,000 drink cans.

Skin, nails and hair

The tough, protective surface of your body is almost entirely dead.

 Every four years you shed your own body weight in dead skin.

 You have about 5 million hairs, but only 100,000 are on your head.

The thickest skin on your body is on the soles of your feet.

Fighting disease

Germs are always trying to get inside you, but your body fights back.

Lassa fever is a very dangerous disease. It kills about a fifth of its victims.

Bacteria are so small that a thousand could fit on the head of a pin.

The world's most common disease is the common cold.

Cancer happens when your own cells multiply out of control.

When you recover from an infectious disease, your body becomes immune to it.

Digestive system

Digestion turns food into simple chemicals that your body can make into new cells or use for fuel.

The food you eat in a year weighs as much as a car.

You make enough spit in your lifetime to fill two swimming pools.

Your digestive glands start working as soon as you smell or see food.

Your tongue senses five tastes: salty, sweet, sour, bitter, and savoury.

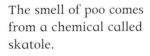
The smell of poo comes from a chemical called skatole.

Each hair on your head grows for about 3 or 4 years and then falls out. A new one grows in its place.

Urinary system

Urine gets rid of chemicals that your body doesn't need.

You will make enough urine in your lifetime to fill 500 baths.

Asparagus can turn your urine green. Blackberries can turn it red.

Reproduction

The reproductive organs create new people from tiny specks of matter.

The most babies born to one mother is 69. Most were twins, triplets, or quads.

The first quintuplets known to have survived infancy were born in 1934.

Growth

As you grow you slowly change into an adult, but it takes a long time!

The fastest-growing part of a baby's body is its head.

A girl is about three-quarters of her adult height at 7 years old.

A boy is about three-quarters of his adult height at 9 years old.

Through the ages

The human body is so amazingly complicated that it's taken doctors at least 4000 years to figure out how it works. Their discoveries have led to many new ways of curing illness.

460–377 BC

The Greek doctor Hippocrates is sometimes called the father of medicine. He was one of the first people to realize that diseases have natural causes and cures.

Before the time of Hippocrates, many people thought that diseases were punishments sent by the gods.

 250 BC Egyptian doctors cut open corpses to find out how the body works.

 100 BC Chinese doctors discover that blood travels around the body in cycles.

 1290 Spectacles are worn for the first time in Venice, Italy.

 **1350** Rats spread bubonic plague in Europe, killing a quarter of the people.

 1500 A Swiss pig farmer performs the first Caesarian section on a living person.

 **1596** The Italian scientist Galileo Galilei invents the thermometer.

1684 Dutch microscopist Antony van Leeuwenhoek discovers blood cells.

 1770 The world's first comfortable false teeth are used in France.

 1796 English surgeon Edward Jenner discovers how to make vaccines.

 **1816** The stethoscope is used for the first time.

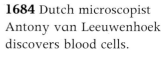

What life-saving antibiotic did Alexander Fleming discover?

The Italian scientist Lazzaro Spallanzani ate his own sick over and over to find out how the stomach works.

 1818 James Blundell carries out the first blood transfusion.

 1852 Doctors use bandages soaked in plaster to make casts.

1853 Scottish doctor Alexander Wood invents the syringe.

 **1895** Wilhelm Röntgen accidentally discovers how to take X-rays of bones.

 1928 An English scientist discovers antibiotics – drugs that kill bacteria.

 1953 Scientists work out the structure of DNA, the chemical that carries genes.

 1955 Doctors start using ultrasound scanners to see babies inside the womb.

 1967 Surgeon Christiaan Barnard carries out the first heart transplant.

 1971 Brain scanners come into use, allowing doctors to study living brains.

 1978 Louise Joy Brown, the first test-tube baby, is born in England.

Modern medicine

Doctors know more about how the body works than ever before, but there are still some mysteries, like why we hiccup or how the brain works.

Glossary

Artery A blood vessel that carries blood away from your heart to the rest of your body.

Bacteria Tiny one-cell creatures found all around us. Some are helpful, others cause diseases.

Blood vessel Any tube that carries blood through your body.

Capillary The smallest type of blood vessel. Your body contains thousands of miles of capillaries.

Cell The smallest living unit of your body.

Diaphragm A strong, flat sheet of muscle under your lungs. You use it when you breathe.

Digestion The process that breaks down food into tiny pieces that your body can absorb and use.

Enzyme A substance that speeds up a particular chemical reaction in the body. Digestive enzymes speed up the breakdown of food molecules.

Epiglottis A trapdoor-like tag of skin that stops food going into your breathing tubes when you swallow.

Oesophagus The tube from your mouth that takes food to your stomach when you swallow.

Genes Instructions that control the way your body develops and works. Genes pass from parents to their children.

Germs Tiny living things that can get into your body and cause illness. Bacteria and viruses are germs.

Gland A group of specialized cells that make and release a particular substance such as a hormone or enzyme.

Hormone A chemical produced by one part of the body in order to change the way a different part of the body works. Hormones are made in glands and carried by the blood.

Joint A connection between two bones.

Mucus Slippery liquid on the inside of your nose, throat, and intestines.

Nerves Threads of tissue that carry high-speed signals around the body.

Nutrients The basic chemicals that make up food. Your body uses nutrients for fuel, growth, and repair.

Organ A group of tissues that form a body part designed for a specific job. Your stomach is an organ.

Oxygen One of the gases in the air. You need to breathe in oxygen to live.

Proteins Vital nutrients that help your body build new cells. Food such as meat, eggs, fish, and cheese are rich in proteins.

Receptor A type of nerve cell that detects a change outside or inside the body, helping to create one of the senses. Touch receptors in the skin, for example, help create the sense of touch.

Reflex A reaction that is out of your control, like breathing or blinking when something gets near your eyes.

Saliva The liquid in your mouth. Saliva helps you taste, swallow, and digest food.

System A group of organs that work together. Your mouth, stomach, and intestines make up your digestive system.

Tissue A group of cells that look and act the same. Muscle is a type of tissue.

Umbilical cord The tube joining a baby to its mother's body while it is still inside her.

Urine Waste liquid that passes out of you when you go to the toilet. Urine is made of water and chemicals your body doesn't need.

Vaccination A substance that is swallowed or injected to protect your body from disease.

Vein A blood vessel that carries blood towards your heart.

Vertebra One of the bones that link together to form your backbone, or spine.

X-rays Invisible rays that pass through objects. X-ray photographs show the inside of your body.

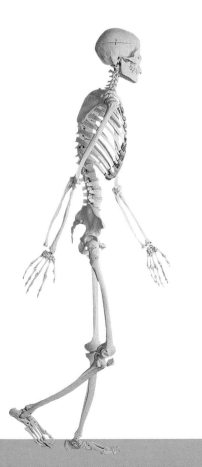
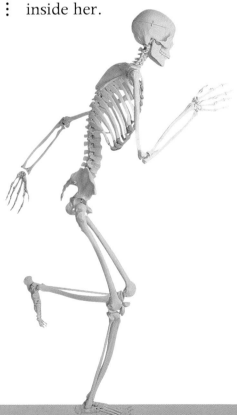
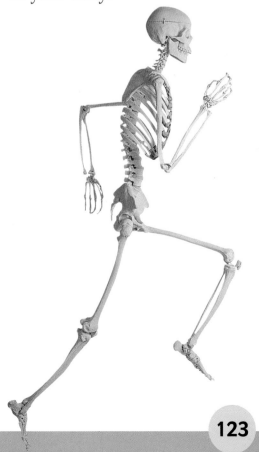

Index

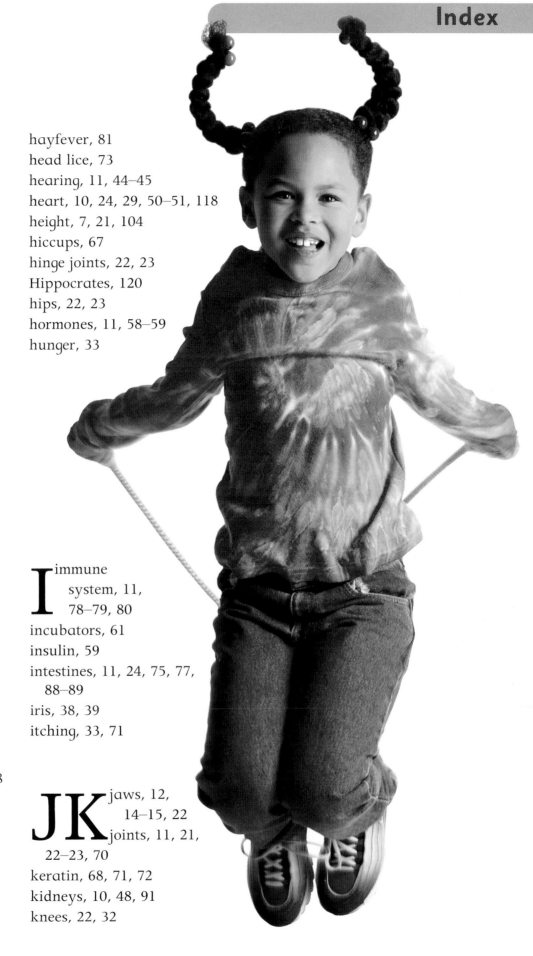

Picture credits

The publisher would like to thank the following for their kind permission to reproduce their images:

(Key: a-above; c-centre; b-below; l-left; r-right; t-top)

4 Corbis: Larry Williams (c); Science Photo Library: (bc); Getty Images: Barbara Peacock (cl). 5 Alamy Images: Aflo Foto Agency (tc), Janine Wiedel Photolibrary (cra), Pictor (cr); Corbis: Reuters (cla), Science Photo Library: (tr), Dr. Gopal Murti (crb), VVG (br). 6 Corbis: Laura Doss. 7 Alamy Images: Goodshoot (tr), Janine Wiedel Photolibrary (tc); Corbis: Jose Luis Pelaez (bl); 8 Science Photo Library: Dr. Gopal Murti (br), Martin Dohrn (cra). 9 Science Photo Library: (jar 3); Andrew Syred (tr), Prof. Aaron Polliack (jar 2), VVG (cl), (jar 1), (jar 4). 10 Alamy Images: RubberBall Productions (r); Corbis: Thom Lang (cl brain) Science Photo Library: J.L. Martra, Publiphoto Diffusion (bl); Victor de Schwanberg (cl heart), (cl kidney). 11 Alamy Images: Ablestock (bl), Comstock Images (button 5); Pictor (t), RubberBall Productions (c), (button 2). 13 DK Images: Oxford University Museum (ca); Science Photo Library: Pascal Goetgheluck (bl). 14 Science Photo Library: Sovereign ISM (bl). 15 Science Photo Library: D. Roberts (bl), Michael Donne, University of Manchester (br). 18 Science Photo Library: Andrew Syred (br), CNRI (cr), VVG (bl). 19 Alamy Images: Medical-on-line (cla); Science Photo Library: (cr), Department of Clinical Radiology, Salisbury District Hospital (tc), VVG (crb). 20 Alamy Images: Superstock (b); Science Photo Library: VVG (cr). 20-21 Science Photo Library: (t). 23 Science Photo Library: Mehua Kulyk (cl); Getty Images: David Roth (crb). 24 Science Photo Library: Astrid & Hans-Frieder Michler (cla), Prof. P. Motta/Dept. of Anatomy/University "La Sapienza" (bl), Victor de Schwanberg (clb), VVG (cl). 25 Corbis: Kevin R. Morris (r). 26 Corbis: (l). 27 Corbis: Tom & Dee Ann McCarthy (clb). 28 Corbis: Ed Bock (tr), Thierry Orban/Sygma (cl); 28-29 Getty Images: Mike Timo. 29 Science Photo Library: Keith, Custom Medical Stock Photo (tl). 30 Getty Images: BodyOnline (c). 31 Corbis: Bryan F. Peterson (crb), Warren Morgan (bl); Colour Vision Store: (crbb); Science Photo Library: Dr. Goran Bredberg (crb), Mehau Kulyk (cra), Nancy Kedersha (tr), Omikron (cr). 32 Corbis: Jim Craigmyle (tl); Science Photo Library: Nancy Kedersha (br). 33 Corbis: Christine Osborne (tr); Science Photo Library: Michael Donne (tl). 34-35 Corbis: Norbert Schaefer (c). 35 Science Photo Library: Joe Bator (cb). 36 ImageState/Pictor: StockImage (cl); Science Photo Library: Omikron (br). 37 Science Photo Library: CNRI (br); Getty Images: Ross Whitaker (tl). 38 Science Photo Library: Gusto (bl). 40 Corbis: Lee White (background). 41 Alamy Images: BananaStock (br); 41 Corbis: Lee White (ca), (c); Colour Vision Store: (tr); 41 Science Photo Library: David Becker (cl). 42 DK Images: Natural History Museum (button 5); Science Photo Library: Mehau Kulyk (l). 44 Getty Images: Ross Whitaker (br). 46 Corbis: Tom Stewart (r). 47

Corbis: Dave G. Houser (tr), Firefly Productions (cb); Science Photo Library: Dr. Goran Bredberg (bc). 49 Science Photo Library: Susumu Nishinaga (tc). 51 Science Photo Library: CNRI (crb), Dr. P. Marazzi (br), NIBSC (cra), (cr). 52 Science Photo Library: Susumu Nishinaga (br), VVG (cr). 53 Science Photo Library: NIBSC (cl). 54 Science Photo Library: BSPI, Gilles (bl), Professors P.M. Motta & S. Correr (tl); Roger Harris (cb). 54-55 Science Photo Library: Dr. Yogas Nikas (b). 55 Science Photo Library: (tl), NIBSC (tr), Roger Harris (c). 56 Corbis: Tom Stewart (bl); Science Photo Library: CNRI (cr). 57 Alamy Images: Shout (button 1); Photolibrary.com: Leanne Temme (cl); Science Photo Library: Alex Bartel (button 4), Astrid & Hanns-Frieder Michler (button 3), Martin Dohrn (tl). 58 Getty Images: Erin Patrice O'Brien (b). 63 Corbis: Stephen Frink (cr); Science Photo Library: David M. Martin M.D. (cla), Mark Thomas (tl), Matt Meadows, Peter Arnold Inc. (br), Proff. Motta, Correr & Nottola/University "La Sapienza", Rome (crb). 64 Science Photo Library: Hank Morgan (cra). 65 Bubbles: Ian West (cl); Corbis: Don Mason (tl), Paul A. Souders (br); Getty Images: Stephanie Rausser (ca). 66 Science Photo Library: Damien Lovegrove (l), Matt Meadows, Peter Arnold Inc. (tr), Proff. Motta, Correr & Nottola/University "La Sapienza", Rome (cr). 68 Alamy Images: Phoebe Dunn (cra); Science Photo Library: Andrew Syred (crb), (br); VVG (c). 69 Alamy Images: Pixland (tl). ImageState/Pictor: (bl). 70 Science Photo Library: VVG (bc). 71 Science Photo Library: Andrew Syred (ca); Lauren Shear (bc); Getty Images: Daniel J. Cox (tr). 72 Science Photo Library: VVG (ca). 73 Science Photo Library: Alex Bartel (tr), Martin Dohrn (c), VVG (br), (background). 74 DK Images: AMNH (tr blue), (tr green); Science Photo Library: Dr. Jeremy Burgess (br); Getty Images: Suzanne ann Nick Geary (bl). 75 DK Images: AMNH (button 1); Photolibrary.com: OSF (tr); Science Photo Library: Dr. Kari Lounatamaa (cla), Eye of Science (br), John Hadfield (cb). 76 Science Photo Library: Biophoto Associates (cl), Custom Medical Stock Photo (tc), Prof P.Motta/Dept of Anatomy/University, "La Sapienza", Rome (br). 77 Science Photo Library: CNRI (bc), Professoers P.M. Motta, K.R. Porter & P.M. Andrews (ca). 78 DK Images: AMNH (tr); Science Photo Library: Biology Media (br). 79 Science Photo Library: BSIP Estiot (tr); Getty Images: Chris Harvey (cl), Steven Peters (tl). 80 Corbis: Paul A. Souders (cl); Science Photo Library: Andrew Syred (button 4), Dr. Jeremy Burgess (button 1), K.H. Kjeldsen (b). 81 Corbis: Lester V. Bergman (cla); Getty Image: Digital Vision (br); Science Photo Library: Dr. Jeremy Burgess (tr), Dr. P. Marazzi (cr), Mark Clarke (bc). 83 Science Photo Library: BSIP, Cavallini James (crb), David

M. Martin M.D. (br) Gusto Productions (cra), VVG (cr). 84 Corbis: Michael Keller (car); Powerstock: age fotostock (tl); Science Photo Library: Gusto Productions (tr). 85 Science Photo Library: Hattie Young (tl). 86 Science Photo Library: Dr. P. Marazzi (bl), Tek Image (tl), VVG (c). 87 Science Photo Library: David. M. Martin M.D. (c); Zefa Visual Media: Chad Johnston/Masterfile (l). 88 Science Photo Library: David M. Martin M.D. (c) Eye of Science (cl). 89 Science Photo Library: David M. Martin M.D. (cr). 92 Science Photo Library: (c), (cr), BSIP, Cavallini James (tr). 93 Alamy Images: Robert Harding (tr). 94 Robert Harding Picture Library: (c). Science Photo Library: Christian Darkin (tr). 95 Science Photo Library: Dr. Yorgos Nikas (tl), (tc), (tr). 96 Penny Arlon: (ca); Mother & Baby Picture Library: Ian Hooton (tr); Photolibrary.com: OSF (br); Science Photo Library: Dr. G. Moscoso (bl), Edelmann (bc). 97 Alamy Images: BM2 (tl); Photolibrary.com: OSF (tr); Getty Images: Ross Whitaker (bc). 98 Getty Images: (c). 98-99 Alamy Images: Big Cheese Photo (b). 99 Alamy Images: Robert Llewellyn (tr); Corbis: Brooks Kraft (br). 101 Corbis: Strauss/Curtis (tl). 102 Corbis: O'Brien Productions (cl). 103 Corbis: Larry Williams (r); Rex Features: Phanie Agency/PHN (tl). 104 Corbis: Pete Saloutos cl. 104-105 Science Photo Library: Alfred Pasieka (t), Blustone (b). 105 Corbis: Roy Morsch (tr); Getty Images: Yann Layma (tl). 107 Corbis: Norbert Schaefer (cl). 109 Science Photo Library: Oscar Burnell (br); Zefa Visual Media: Robert Karpa/Masterfile (tc). 110 ImageState/Pictor: (tl), (cr). 111 Science Photo Library: Adam Hart-Davis (tc), Michael Donne (br), Pascal Goetgheluck (clb). 113 Corbis: Ariel Skelley (cl); Getty Images: Erin Patrice O'Brien (b). 114 Getty Images: Ian Sanderson (tr). 117 Corbis: Mark Tuschman (c); Getty Images: Tim Flach (tl). 118 Science Photo Library: Astrid & Hanns-Frieder Michler (button 1). 119 DK Images: Judith Miller/Elms Letsers (button 1); Science Photo Library: Dr. Tony Brain (button 2). 120 DK Images: British Museum (button 1), Judith Miller/TW conroy (button 9). 121 Corbis: Larry Williams (button 4), Michael Pole (r); Science Photo Library: (button 4), Edelmann (button 7), Victor de Schwanberg (button 8). 125 Alamy Images: RubberBall Productions. 126-127 Alamy Images: Aflo Foto Agency

All other images © Dorling Kindersley
www.dkimages.com

Acknowledgements

Dorling Kindersley would like to thank: Elinor Greenwood, Lorrie Mack, and Fleur Star for editorial assistance, Dorian Spencer Davies for additional illustration, Mary Sandberg for additional design assistance, Julia Harris-Voss for picture research, and Chris Bernstein for compiling the index.

The end